MASS COMMUNICATIONS

EDITED BY

WILLIAM P. LINEBERRY

THE H. W. WILSON COMPANY

NEW YORK   1969

THE REFERENCE SHELF

The books in this series contain reprints of articles, excerpts from books, and addresses on current issues and social trends in the United States and other countries. There are six separately bound numbers in each volume, all of which are generally published in the same calendar year. One number is a collection of recent speeches; each of the others is devoted to a single subject and gives background information and discussion from various points of view, concluding with a comprehensive bibliography.

Subscribers to the current volume receive the books as issued. The subscription rate is $14 in the United States and Canada ($17 foreign) for a volume of six numbers. Single numbers are $3.50 each in the United States and Canada ($4 foreign).

MASS COMMUNICATIONS
Copyright © 1969
By The H. W. Wilson Company
Standard Book Number 8242-0108-6
Library of Congress Catalog Card Number 69-15809

PRINTED IN THE UNITED STATES OF AMERICA

PREFACE

Can man stay emotionally abreast of his own intellectual precocity? That has become a central question of the twentieth century. And in few areas is the issue more dramatically posed than in that of mass communications. Over the last half century man's capacity to communicate with his fellow men has grown by leaps and bounds—radio, television, the transistor, communications satellites—until at last a worldwide communications grid embracing all of mankind is in the offing. But, given these wondrous products of man's scientific ingenuity, what have men to say to each other? Will the content of communication match the brilliance of its techniques?

There are many among us who have already answered a resounding *no* to that question. They look at the way in which mass communications techniques are being applied in America, and they see, in the words of one former member of the Federal Communications Commission, a "vast wasteland." Television, radio, the newspapers, magazines—all have come under attack for failing to live up to their potential. The message, in short, has not been at all equal to the medium, as far as these critics are concerned.

Others are more optimistic. For them the revolution in communications has ushered in a new era in man's history. It is already estimated that nine out of ten homes in the United States possess one or more television receivers. An even higher percentage have radios. This means, for one thing, that the President of the United States can instantaneously communicate with virtually every man, woman, and child in the nation on the great issues of public policy. It means that the great drama of human history—the wars, the rebellions, the reach for the moon and stars, the discoveries of science and medicine—unfolds in our living rooms, frequently before our very eyes. Under the impact of such remarkable developments, the old parochialisms are breaking down. All men are truly becoming citizens of the world.

This compilation is designed to explore the status of mass communications in America today—their impact on society, their achievements and shortcomings, and their potential for the future. The first section examines the impact of the mass media, for good or ill, on our daily lives. Are violence and civil disorder really as "American as cherry pie," or do the media exploit these phenomena to society's detriment? And, what do the self-appointed prophets of communications—for example, Marshall McLuhan—have to say about the media's role in shaping modern society?

The next section turns to a survey of current trends in the mass media, from the promise of communications satellites to the role of radio in the suburbs to the emergence of an "underground press" catering to the alienated among our middle-class youth. In the third section, some of the controversies currently besetting the mass media are discussed—television's handling of the news, the drive for profits and its impact on broadcasting and publishing, and the dangers posed by concentrated ownership and control of the nation's airwaves.

The fourth and final section peers briefly into the future. Will worldwide three-dimensional TV in every room be our fate? How will man apply the technological advances of the future? Will national boundaries melt under the impact of a worldwide communications grid?

The mass media have become a central part of our lives. They influence us in ways yet unknown, and their potential for good or ill staggers even the modern scientific imagination. This compilation seeks to draw the media into perspective and survey the problems and opportunities they pose for our time.

The compiler wishes to thank the authors and publishers who have courteously granted permission for the reprinting of their materials in this book. He is indebted to Stephanie Lineberry and Carolyn Dranoff for their able assistance in the preparation of the manuscript.

WILLIAM P. LINEBERRY

May 1969

CONTENTS

I. THE IMPACT ON SOCIETY

EDITOR'S INTRODUCTION

Precisely what Marshall McLuhan means when he says that "the medium is the message" is still a mystery to many people, but almost everyone would agree that the mass media are having a profound effect on society as a whole. In fact, as Wesley C. Clark, the dean of Syracuse University's School of Journalism, points out in the first article in this compilation, "Most of the sins of America today are charged to mass communications."

However unfair such blanket charges may be, nobody doubts that the media are influential in shaping our thoughts, deeds, and lives. Ask any advertiser. The issue is not *whether* mass communications are affecting our society; everyone agrees that they are—and profoundly. The issue is rather *how and in what ways* they are and should be affecting our lives.

There are some who charge, for example, that we are living in a "sick society," rife with crime, violence, and civil disorder. Can any or all of these phenomena be traced to the impact of mass communications? Does the violence of a TV western, for instance, project itself into our streets as well as our living rooms? Do racial strife and campus confrontations feed on television coverage?

This section explores the impact of mass communications on America today and some of the controversies surrounding that impact. First, Dean Clark traces the role of mass communications in shaping America's history and lends perspective to some current assessments. The next two articles take up the hotly debated issue of violence in the media and its relation, if any, to the violence in American life. In the first of these articles a professor of communications at the Graduate School of Yeshiva University argues that the Kennedy-King-Kennedy assassinations have put mass communications on trial, as well as the alleged slayers. In the second of the articles the television critic for *Commentary* magazine contends that "the cult of violence is based upon something far more serious than the desire of a few cynical men to get rich by pandering to base appetites."

The last two articles in this section explore the meaning of Marshall McLuhan, who has grown famous seeking to explore the meaning of mass communications in our society as a whole. Is he a brilliantly original thinker or a sham? Both views are presented.

A FORCE FOR CHANGE AND CHALLENGE [1]

Most of the sins of America today are charged to mass communications. In fact, whole academic disciplines have been built on this assumption. The fact is that most of the sins credited to the mass media have been committed by others and the real sins of the mass media, like their accomplishments, have gone unheralded. Let me explain.

The impact of mass communications in America has been persistent, consistent, and with us for more than one hundred years now. The mass media have changed the face of America, in some ways for the better and in some ways for the worse, some obvious and some not so obvious. The mass media have been given some credit for a great many of these changes, but some are hardly credited to them at all, and yet it is they—the mass media—who are largely responsible for much of the social legislation which now affects your lives and mine.

[1] From "The Impact of Mass Communications in America," by Wesley C. Clark, dean, School of Journalism, Syracuse University. *Annals of the American Academy of Political and Social Science.* 378:68-74. Jl. '68. Reprinted by permission.

The Impact of Mass Media in the Past

When people speak today of mass communications and of the mass media, they think of audiences in terms of hundreds, and perhaps even thousands, of millions. But one hundred years ago, when this country was more sparsely populated, circulations of newspapers were not in the millions. Nevertheless, the great newspapers and magazines which existed in those days were, by almost any standards, mass media, engaged in mass communications. They were directed to the masses. They were read by the masses, and, presumably, they had some effect on the masses.

For instance, Horace Greeley's *Tribune* never had a circulation of 300,000. But it was read throughout the United States, and the admonitions of Mr. Greeley were listened to and debated throughout the United States.

The mass media of those days were responsible for crystallizing the nation's opinions about the abolition of slavery and about the kinds of amendments to the Constitution which grew out of Abraham Lincoln's statement that all men are created equal. Without the newspapers' presentation of this point of view for ten or fifteen years, it is inconceivable that Lincoln would have made such a statement, and unlikely that the Civil War would have occurred when it did—and perhaps it might not have happened at all.

This is not to attribute to today's mass media and to the newspapers and magazines of the late nineteenth century all of the political and social changes which have come about in the American scene. The pulpit, the Chautauqua—that early-day version of television—and all of the other means of communication—which were available in those days helped to create this atmosphere. Nevertheless, no serious historian of the times can deny the important role of the mass media in changing America.

With this in mind, a look at history reveals a number of other things for which the mass media were largely responsible. The muckrakers of the late nineteenth century and early twentieth century—public figures such as Ida Tarbell, Lincoln Steffens, and others—were aided and abetted by newspapers and magazines across the land, and thus were largely responsible for the first early restrictions imposed upon business in this country. No Judge Landis could have come to the conclusion that the great monopoly of the Standard Oil Company should be broken up, had he not been so conditioned and so impressed by the press that such a decision was made easily possible. Nor can we deny the place of the nation's press in building the pressure which made it possible for the Congress of the United States to adopt the kind of legislation which eventually resulted in the Standard Oil cases getting into the courts. To be sure, Teddy Roosevelt and others were trustbusters in those days, but these were men who were coursing a sea of sentiment created by mass magazine and mass newspaper stories over a period of twenty or thirty years. . . .

Contemporary Mass Media's Effects on Society

This, perhaps, is ancient history. What are the mass media doing now, and what have they done recently, to change the face of America, or have they rather been merely carping critics of the changes which have come about?

One of the massive changes in the American scene has been the rise of the labor unions to positions of power. It is now apparent that the restrictions imposed upon business by various laws, and by the courts, have resulted in business' having little real power in the American political scene. It is also apparent that while government has risen to new heights of power and control, the only serious challenge to these powers is provided by the labor unions, who defy the government again and again, even when laws and sanctions have been reduced to a minimum.

How did this come about? It came about because for more than fifty years the press of this country, largely the newspapers, pleaded the cause of labor in a multitude of ways. They gave publicity to Sacco and Vanzetti, to Tom

Mooney, to all of the complaints against the crimes of management. They made folk heroes out of labor union leaders such as John L. Lewis of the United Mine Workers, Walter Reuther of the Congress of Industrial Organizations, Samuel Gompers of the American Federation of Labor, Eugene Debs of the American Railway Union, and a host of others. They created a climate which made it possible for legislators to pass, and for executive branches to approve, legislation favoring labor. This is apparent in the laws of both the Federal and state governments. It is apparent in the executive branch of the government, and it is even apparent in the judicial branch of the government. There is no need to cite the host of administrative rules or the flux of Supreme Court decisions which bear out this point.

But, in a sense, these are the obvious things which grew out of the creation by the mass media of a climate of opinion favorable to social change in America. There are many obvious changes in which the mass media played a decisive, although unheralded, role.

Social historians of the present and recent American scene give little or no credit to the role of the mass media in making possible the Social Security Act. . . .

Franklin D. Roosevelt and the New Deal were merely the mechanism which put into being an American dream which had been sold to the American people for some seventy-five years by the great insurance companies; for during that time, insurance companies had preached the necessity for security in old age. "Make sure you have enough insurance to take care of your family." "Take out an annuity to take care of your old age." These are not new slogans; these are not Social Security slogans; these have been the slogans of insurance companies ever since life insurance and annuity insurance began to play a role in the United States. . . .

Again, Medicaid and Medicare are the result, not of the wild-eyed dreams of some politician, but of the mass propaganda of various insurance businesses, told through the media of the newspapers, the magazines, radio, and television, and drummed into the American people for the last twenty years.

With all of this propaganda, these persuasive methods, and with the climate of opinion thereby created, it would be incredible if politicians had not seized upon these slogans or ideas and incorporated them into their platforms and then into law.

There are a number of other areas in which the mass media have changed the face of America with the aid and active participation of politicians. Thus, for instance, the jewel in the crown of the Kennedy administration—the Peace Corps—is a direct development of the widespread interest of the mass communicators in the missionaries of America. For more than one hundred years, the role of the missionaries in bettering the lot of people in the underdeveloped areas was the subject of a great many articles and of books. The principal criticism of the missionaries came from the fact that they were engaged in selling Christianity abroad. And we have such plays as Somerset Maugham's *Rain* and the like which sharpened this criticism considerably. But there was no question in many people's minds that the missionaries had done a considerable amount of good in alleviating the ills of mankind in foreign countries. The Peace Corps, thus, was something that was difficult for any politician to deny, once the idea of a missionary society without God, or with a multitude of gods, was conceived.

Again, the mass media's gilding of the glories of private charity, in all of its aspects, made it difficult for any politician to deny that an increase in the scope of public welfare was necessary.

The Impact of Social Change on the Mass Media

The great media of mass communications do not stand alone, untouched by the other forces which are changing our society. They not only shape our society; they are shaped by it. And as society changes the mass media, so it, in turn, is changed by them.

The factors which have had the most effect in changing the nation are its increasing population, its increasing mobility, and the almost astronomical increase in the area of the public interest.

As more and more people have come to populate the nation and as their mobility has increased tremendously, the public interest has, of necessity, widened and broadened. Where once the disposal of waste was a private matter—the head of the household buried the waste in the backyard or fed it to the pigs—now waste is no longer a private matter, nor solely the concern of a town or a county, but has become a Federal concern. Again, where once the wage contract between the employer and the employee was a private arrangement, now the Federal Government has stepped in and regulates such arrangements.

Confronted with these increases in population and in mobility and the consequent enormous increase in the areas of public interest, the media of mass communication have been swamped with an increase in news. For wherever the citizen and the public interest meet—in crime, in zoning, in food regulations, in labor matters, and in thousands of other places where the law and the people meet—these events must be reported if the people of the nation are to have the kind of information that they need in order to govern themselves properly.

In the face of the enormous and increasing need for news, the media of mass communications find themselves limited by the mind of man himself. It becomes a question of just how much time and attention he will devote to finding out about his environment through the mass media. Newspapers find that generally a man will devote thirty or forty minutes a day to reading the newspaper. Radio and television find that fifteen, or at most thirty, minutes comprise the outer limit of listening to or watching Huntley and Brinkley. In thirty or forty minutes, a man can read fifteen thousand to forty thousand words. In the same thirty minutes, he can listen to three thousand words, or about four newspaper columns.

This very fact tends to limit the amount of news which is published in the great newspapers and magazines, and limits even more severely the amount of news which is available through radio and television.

Higher Thresholds of Attention

Thus, newspapers everywhere have tended to raise the thresholds of their attention. Even so, thresholds of radio and television are even higher, and of necessity must be higher.

That this rise in the thresholds of attention of the mass communicators has had a profound influence on the structure of our government is suggested by two illustrations—one concerned with the courts, and the other concerned with the legislative and executive branches of the government.

A recent study of a county containing more than 400,000 people indicated that in a single month there were two thousand court cases of all kinds—Federal, state, county, and municipal—all of them available for reporting by the mass media. The same study showed that the two daily newspapers which serve the county printed stories about less than sixty of these cases. In more populous areas, the figures would be even more astounding.

That the press does not report more court cases is due to the constant pressure to raise the thresholds of their attention. Thus, for most people, we have established an unofficial system of secret courts. The courts, the bar associations, and the legislatures are now trying to provide a court system whose secrecy is officially instead of unofficially sanctioned. And this is despite the fact that if the history of civilization proves nothing else, it proves that where secrecy cloaks the use of power it also cloaks the abuse of power. The consequence of this judicial secrecy, official and unofficial, is a growing distrust by people everywhere of the courts, the judiciary, the legal profession, and the mass media.

The impact of the rising thresholds of attention of the mass media upon the legislative and executive branches of the government is best illustrated by the great metropolitan area of New York City, where some twenty congressmen are elected every two years. These are United States congressmen—not dog wardens or local constables—but twenty members of that august body which enacts the laws of the United States. Yet, in campaign after campaign, the New York City papers in years past, and I suspect even in . . . [1968] devote, in the six weeks preceding an election, as few as five hundred words to each congressional candidate and, unless the congressional candidate is a John Lindsay, hardly more than that. As a matter of fact, most New Yorkers are unaware of the congressional district in which they live or of the congressman who, presumably, represents them.

In these circumstances, it is not important to be an outstanding congressman or to represent a particular district well. But it is important to be a member of a winning political party and to ride on the coattails of that party. Thus, more and more, for the metropolitan congressmen, the question of survival depends, not upon their own efforts, but upon the efforts and the image presented by the leader of the party—in short, the President of the United States, or the governor of the state. . . .

And as the arena of meaningful political action moves more and more toward Washington, and as secrecy cloaks the actions of more and more areas of government, the political man in America becomes more and more frustrated and tempted to forgo political action. . . . To ask a political man to be informed through the mass media about government in depth and in detail when he has little or no chance to use the information to change the course of government is to ask too much.

By raising the thresholds of their attention to unprecedented heights, the mass media of communications have both simplified and complicated American life. They have simplified it by making it easy to concentrate upon a few great political leaders. They have complicated it by making it impossible for many individuals to be heard when the mechanisms of society impinge abrasively upon their rights and their lives. They have also complicated it to the extent that if individuals or groups have problems which need to be brought to the attention of the public, they must hire public relations counsel to make sure that the things that they need are brought to the attention of the public, or they must create some kind of a disturbance to make their needs known to the great mass media—or perhaps they must do both: hire public relations counsel to organize riots.

Summary

To summarize, then: mass communications and the mass media have played a major role in changing the face of America; they are playing a major role; they will continue to do so.

The mass media, by their very nature, by the limitations imposed upon them by man and by a changing society, are challenging the basic assumptions upon which this government was erected.

They have given us instant nationwide fashions and modes, and perhaps instant heroes, or nonheroes, both political and nonpolitical.

They have contributed substantially to the frustrations, political and otherwise, which beset the American populace.

But they have also, and in this lies the hope of America, paved the way for the great pieces of social legislation which have made this nation a better place in which to live.

DOES VIOLENCE BREED VIOLENCE? [2]

Many of our national leaders and social critics who have called for an examination of violence in America have em-

[2] From "Violence in the Mass Media," by Solomon Simonson, professor of communications at the Graduate School of Yeshiva University, New York City, and author of Crisis in Television. Catholic World. 207:264-8. S. '68. Reprinted by permission.

phasized the distressing stimuli of the mass media. But their references have been directed chiefly to the media's functions as escape jets of vicarious thrills, as open conduits of information, as mirrors of reality—characteristics of mere conveyers rather than of producers of violence—and it is difficult to see how such attributes can be considered to be the basis for a real case against the media. Nevertheless, the recurrence of tragedy in the assassinations of Kennedy, King, and Kennedy, has ignited public suspicion to the point where few people are willing to exonerate press, films, and television without some sort of trial.

For those who were convinced of the media's mischief before the killing of President Kennedy—persons we shall identify as members of a B.A. (Before Assassination) group —a foreshadowing of tragedy, if not a direct forewarning, was explicitly demonstrated in the films *The Manchurian Candidate* and *Suddenly*. In *Manchurian Candidate,* we were introduced to a weak and suggestible creature as he is brainwashed and hypnotized in order to assassinate a leading political figure. *Suddenly* goes still further by focusing on a sniper who is heading a gang-conspiracy for assassination. The highlights of the two films are in the scenes depicting "how practice makes perfect" in the arts of rifle-sighting in the commission of the crimes.

The A.A.-1 group—those who after the assassination of President Kennedy suddenly realized that there was a mad resemblance between *Suddenly* and Dallas—began to clamor for some kind of inquiry into the influence of the media.

In the meantime, the public was becoming aware also of a pattern in the assassinations. As noted by President Johnson, the ten major killings in the nation reveal to a dispassionate observer that seven of them were of civil rights workers and leaders, while two others, the Kennedy brothers, were formidable leaders in the struggle for equal rights for all citizens, and only one, Rockwell, was killed in an intraorganizational struggle.

Yellow Journalism Revisited

The A.A.-2 group—those who after the assassination of Martin Luther King noted this pattern in the assassinations, a pattern that smelled of conspiracy, a pattern that spelled white backlash criminality—grew wary of the enthusiastic reportage of criminal behavior in the newspapers which described in both gory and gloried terms the trivial details of every crime.

While some of the newspapers have scrupulously been avoiding a trend to yellow journalism, the periodicals have picked up this slack and joined the old game of "exposing the private escapades" of criminals and other nonnewsworthy creatures. After its lesson with Oswald, television had turned its lens away from inquiry and coverboy glorification of the alleged murderer of Senator Kennedy. The periodical has stepped in where television had pulled out. How true it is that fools step in where angels fear to tread. In its June 21 [1968] issue, *Life* gave front-page coverage to two photographs of Ray and Sirhan balancing the title of its feature article, "The Two Accused." Since *accused* is a semantically neutral or even favorable term and the two pictures, however untouched, depict a forthright eye-contact in one and a distraught pitiable countenance in the other, what ray of human kindness may not go out toward them? The stories show these men to be victims of poor family and society relations, etc. Now, what greater nonsense and immorality can prevail than in such cool glorifications?

The A.A.-3 group—those who, after the assassination of Senator Kennedy, were witnesses to this main feature in *Life* and had their eyes opened in shock at the low abyss of yellow journalism to which some periodicals had sunk—now demanded to know to what lengths a deranged mind would go to attain such world-shaking and rationalized martyrdom.

The weeds of both the *news* and *entertainment* media have spread throughout the land like the plague, and in both cases the roots are readily discoverable. The entertain-

ment media have identified drama with conflict, and the
news media have defined newsworthy as the unusual. Conflict is translated as action, and action is equated with violence. The unusual is identified with turmoil, and excitement
has become synonymous with violence. Both entertainment
and news media thus make violence their prime test for inclusion in their content. Hard-core news of crime represents
the precinct reporter's job as he chases after the police blotter
from town to town. Hard-core pornography . . . coupled with
cool sadism has become the stock-in-trade of the film and
television writer.

There is nothing more pretentious or misleading than
the impression cast by some social critics to the effect that
the American people were formed from the onset of our
history into this mold of violence, that the cult of the gun
governed our rise in power, that it is simply an extension
of overaggressiveness that manifests itself so cruelly and
regularly upon our national consciousness.

The history of the content of the mass media in the last
thirty years puts the lie to these notions. A comparison of
the films of the thirties with those of the sixties indicates
clearly that the "practical" gun has attained prominence
only in recent years. The western was legendary, belonging
to another time. And the detective story has indeed undergone great change from *The Thin Man* to Mike Hammer.
Even the gangster melodramas culminated in ethical resolutions that were both true and reasonable. *Scarface, Public
Enemy* and *Little Caesar* depicted the ugliness of the central
figures without recourse to false sentimentality. Paul Muni,
James Cagney, and Edward G. Robinson were perceived as
actors and not as embodiments of the criminals they por-
trayed so effectively. Their heroism was a result of their act-
ing talents. The contrast to the sixties is striking. What began
in this decade as James Bond spoofing has evolved into *A
Fistful of Dollars, Bonnie and Clyde,* and violence for its
own sake. Even the standards of mystery films have deterio-
rated from Hitchcock's *39 Steps* to his *Psycho. . . .*

When we look at the acclaim that the Academy Awards have granted to some of the film industry's products and personnel, we see that we have taken a long downward trek from Bette Davis' *Dangerous* to Julie Christie's *Darling,* from the characterization of female impishness to nymphomania, from some deceitfulness to any utter lack of values. This seems clear when the majority of the films nominated for the best of the year in 1967 involved violence of one kind or another.

Violence on TV

The advertisers of the films have been making an effort to outdo the films themselves. Recently, the marquee of a theater on New York City's celebrated thoroughfare, Broadway, read as follows: "Taylor, Brando in *Reflections in a Golden Eye.* Lust, nudity, brutality, hatred, and insanity that culminate in murder" (*The Daily News*). What an insidious joining of forces of the press, the film, and the advertiser! Down the block, the picture *Devil's Angels* had this description on the marquee: "See every brutal torture known—bold, inconceivable, shocking, true—violence their god, lust their law." In the thirties, advertising still used the naïve superlatives of colossal, stupendous, magnificent, memorable, and spectacular. When Humphrey Bogart played in *The Left Hand of God,* the advertisement for the film had a gun drawn into the letter *O* of the word God. It was sacrilegious, but not at all as horrendous as "violence their god."

Although television's violence is not of the Grand Guignol variety [Grand Guignol is a small theatre in the Montmartre section of Paris specializing in one- and two-act plays, especially horror plays], a survey reveals that a modicum of violence is an integral part of more than 70 per cent of the programs in prime time. Now, it is questionable whether such programing is truly representative of our times; consequently, it is impossible to defend, either on ethical or logical grounds, this use of the people's airwaves. Clearly, the people need protection from harassment and inundation with violence. But neither the FCC [Federal Communications Commission] nor the self-regulation of the industry is providing it. The FCC will not "censor" and the "telegogs" [i.e., the leaders of the television industry] will not interfere with "creative integrity."

But exercising responsibility is neither censorship nor interference. Mr. [Kenneth A.] Cox and Mr. [Nicholas] Johnson of the FCC have shown signs of being prepared to act on behalf of the people, and the presidents of the networks have promised action. As a result, one of the networks, NBC, has ordered the elimination of violence from promotional material and opening teasers and has changed a basic policy directive from "violence only where justified" to "violence only when essential."

Promises—promises. After the death of Senator Kennedy, the networks courteously displaced shows of "violence" with quieter programs. It may be remembered, also, that out of respect for the death of Valerie Percy, the murdered daughter of Senator Percy of Illinois, CBS removed *Psycho* and substituted *Kings Go Forth* for its Friday night movie. (This happened to have been the evening of Yom Kippur—the holiest day of the Jewish calendar.) The programs of that night included bits of violence in "The Man From UNCLE," "T.H.E. Cat," *Twelve O'Clock High,* and a Milton Berle slapstick on the bitter play, *Who's Afraid of Virginia Woolf. Psycho* caught up to the race by being scheduled later in the year. Sooner or later, promises notwithstanding, tragedies and awesome days notwithstanding, the "telegogs" go back to "business as usual." The addiction to violence will not be cured by promises. Nor will a shift of blame onto the audiences help the situation any. The standard attack of the "telegogs" has been that the people speak through the ratings and that shows of violence have done exceedingly well in the ratings. Drew Pearson wrote of "the American passion for televised crimes and violence," and the Attorney General of the United States, Mr. [Ramsey] Clark, agreed with him on the June 9 program of "Issues and Answers," that television gives people "what they want to see."

Eight Fallacies About TV Violence

The fallacies involved in this position are legion:

1. Among the greatest audiences ever assembled for television programs were for the specials, *The Bridge on the River Kwai, Death of a Salesman, Peter Pan,* etc. These programs beat all their competition in the ratings. The highest attendance and income for any in film history was secured by nonviolent *The Sound of Music.*

2. The demand did not create a supply of these brilliantly styled films with moral insights and objectives. Neither the television nor the film industries continued "to give the people what they wanted to see."

3. In entertainment, it is a more acceptable truism to assert that "the supply creates the demand." Leisure time cries for fulfillment. When we are stimulated in any one direction, we tend to channel our tastes in that direction.

4. Even if the case were otherwise, and the people were responding favorably to shows of violence, the instruments of measuring preference, the ratings, are insufficient to tell the real preferences of people, particularly where the available programs may all be of a similar content and style.

5. Ratings do not inform us of the degree of interest in viewing a program, the composition of the audience, whether the person who is tuned in likes the program, etc.

6. The ratings provide even less evidence of public preferences when an entertainment program of any quality is set up in competition with an educational program or documentary. This would make for a particularly unfair judgment since the documentary or educational program is frequently produced without the technical skills and without the uses of the significant factors of interest that are necessary for good programing.

7. There is no excuse for excessive violence on television on the forthright moral ground that television is a home product and should be treated as a living room guest of an average family.

8. A final counterquestion should be raised: Why give the public what it wishes? No one may claim the right to determine another's best interests, but we should resolve what is generally detrimental to the public interest irrespective of wishes.

A Release for Aggression?

A second staple argument of the producers of the mass media is that no proof has been adduced to show that fictional violence and news-reports of riots have causal relationships to actual violence and further rioting.

The argument is a spurious one. First there are some evidences of violent programs of a peculiar nature that were repeated in almost identical fashion in real life within a 24-to-48-hour span of the program's showing. The play that showed a subway carload of people besieged and tormented by a pair of morbid hoodlums was repeated in the New York subway three times during a forty-eight-hour period following the television show. Neither before nor after this outburst of subway assaults did there occur any similar such attacks. Secondly, there have been many examples of criminals reporting that television stimulated their impulses to violence. Thirdly, reason dictates that life emulates art. Whatever is depicted on a screen has the immediate potential for emulation. Sex scenes, whether in burlesque houses or film programs, stimulate to sex action. The action can be harmless and even productive where the follow-through is with one's spouse. But the action can also be destructive. Violence, unlike sex, is not emulated normally by most people. But there are some, and unfortunately not a very small number of people, who have had the experience and the spur toward violence. Public policy should guard us from stimulating any such minority of sick minds. Other evidences (that have been paid for handsomely by the industry) have indicated that aggression is siphoned off by the catharsis of viewing violence. This is an irrelevant finding since the siphoning-off process may be immediate with a vast majority of people. For the same findings have indicated that with some people the aggression is stored, and with these the aggression is directed outside of the fictional experience. No test can verify the eventual readiness toward violence induced by constant immersion in viewing all manner of violence.

Vice President Humphrey spoke out boldly in the *Look* issue of July 9 [1968]: "I do know that TV in particular has spread the message of rioting and looting . . . and has literally served as a catalyst to promote even more trouble." TV inherited its shoddy definition of newsworthiness from the press that made the coverage of crime and accidents the hard news of the day. To implement such a definition is an exercise of arrogant selectivity in choice of news. Roy Wilkins and James Farmer have a great deal to offer television audiences, but the TV newsmen are keeping them under wraps because of the relative calm of their contributions to civil rights. Every university in the land, including Columbia University, has a thousand-and-one exciting stories to tell, all newsworthy, but the news syndromes of our times focused only on the Columbia sit-ins and strikes.

The third conventional argument of the "telegogs" is that the classical works of art had all manner of violence in them and that life is not without violence. I have given a reply to this fallacious argument in my book on the industry, *Crisis in Television*:

> *Hamlet* and *War and Peace* are nine tenths hesitation and mental deliberation and one tenth violence. Mike Hammer and *The Untouchables* are nine tenths violence and one tenth setting the stage for violence. . . .

Where Does the Blame Lie?

A fourth argument that has the effect of distracting us from the real issues is shared by the "telegogs" with any number of the scholarly establishments. For the "telegogs," it is a diversionary tactic to discuss the nature of aggression, the reduction of hostility, and the controls required for one's own self-discipline. The psychologists join forces, happily, to discuss these issues over and over again as though this were the problem that confronts us. For the producers of the mass media this is a field day of projecting blame on the educational and religious establishments.

Of course, aggression is a primary motivational force, but aggression is not the problem. Aggression can be channeled into hundreds of positive and socially approved cultural streams. Hostility may be used to halt aggressive actions of an unsocial nature. Hostility may be directed against wrong with the soft reprimand of a gentle minister or with the "fire and brimstone" of an angry educator. The deceptiveness of this side issue pulls us away from understanding and preventing that species of aggression and hostility which is our primary concern—and that is violence.

There is one additional species of violence that was cultivated by the "telegogs." After a score of years in which radio was on the "offensive to be inoffensive," on a fearful lookout to avoid controversy, a relatively sudden transition was effected by television. Controversy is now a "good" and should be encouraged. What television has succeeded in doing, however, is to stir up controversy to the point of verbal violence. The new insult barrage of Joe Pyne and Alan Burke is one step short of the physical altercation. Television programs of this kind succeed in being offensive and rarely achieve any genuine discussion of vital issues.

An extreme example of this kind of discussion was presented by the PBL (Public Broadcast Laboratory) in its inaugural program. Whites and blacks were gathered together. The result was that they were enabled to express their hostilities for one another. The verbal exchanges were sharp and threatening. Even as one lady was narrating the loves of her children and their intermarriage that she favored, others were spurning her love with words of aggression. The moderator sat through the program with very little demand of the participants to make relevant contributions.

The failure of television to organize sound discussions is most disappointing. Verbal diatribe and incipient violence can be prevented by maintaining a discussion in an organized fashion. False values on the nature of entertainment and news have misled us. Fallacious arguments concerning the state of public wishes, the adequacy of proof on the causal relations between mass media programs and violence, the comparison with violence in the classics, and the problems of fundamental aggression, have misguided us. And we are faced with the great question that *Good Housekeeping* posed in its full-page advertisement in the New York *Times* on June 12 [1968]: How did we come to a world—an American world—in which the whole apparatus of communications, so potentially powerful for good and so much more available today for young and old alike, seems to glorify violence and immorality?

TELEVISION AND REALITY—WITH ANOTHER VIEW OF VIOLENCE [3]

"Television *as* Reality" might almost have been a better title for this article. The last five horrific years have clearly demonstrated, if demonstration was necessary, that television is no longer a secondary and contingent factor in American life, but part of the very fabric of corporate existence. That the TV versions of some major events have come to seem more authentic than the unmediated occurrences themselves is due, not merely to repetition and ubiquity, but also to the awesome credibility of whatever is transmitted by that unblinking and apparently dispassionate electronic eye. Yet common sense is surely right (whatever philosophers or com-

[3] From "Television and Reality," by Neil Compton, teacher of English at Sir George Williams University, Montreal, and regular television critic for *Commentary*. *Commentary*. 46:82-6. S. '68. Reprinted from *Commentary*, by permission; copyright © 1968 by the American Jewish Committee.

munications theorists may say) to urge us to be worried about the distortion of reality (or our sense of it) that results from the unavoidable selectivity of the medium. Nowadays, complaints tend to center around television's evident preoccupation with violence, and its "white, racist bias." Opinions may and do differ about the significance and justice of these charges, but not even Marshall McLuhan (I like to think) would dismiss them as totally irrelevant. [Marshall McLuhan is the communications theorist whose views are discussed in the following two articles.—Ed.]

How TV Influences Our Lives

Even if public indignation and ritualistic self-incrimination by television executives and producers did not invite comment, a review of the past few months could hardly avoid trying to come to grips with this subject. The triumphs of Eugene McCarthy, the Têt offensive, the decision of the President not to seek reelection, the death and burial of Martin Luther King and Robert Kennedy, and the eruption into riot of scores of American cities were all phenomena which either could not have happened at all before the video age, or would have happened in a very different way. To have ignored all this in favor of such interesting but less urgent topics as the motherless family in serial drama and situation comedy, or the clash of cultures in "Celebrity Billiards," would have been easier than trying to come to grips with what I suspect are insoluble problems. Nonetheless, it would have been a dereliction of duty.

Does American television deliberately and cynically exploit violence for profit? The charge has been frequently made, and seems to be striking home, because all the networks have recently made pious resolutions to change their ways. (Whether any real reformation will take place may be doubted.) Being an old-fashioned, rather bourgeois soul, I find the cult of violence in contemporary culture (whether high or low) both repellent and boring, and I have minimal respect for the intelligence and good faith of those who control commercial television. Nevertheless, I think they deserve to be defended against this particular charge.

The fact is that violence in popular art is nothing new. The Scottish border ballads, much of the Elizabethan drama, Smollett's novels, and Gothick horror tales, all in their different ways testify to this enduring human fascination. In the twentieth century, the United States media certainly have no monopoly in this field: no American series ever exploited death and torture with such kinky and inhuman stylishness as "The Avengers," made in Britain. Oddly enough, the admirers of Steed and Mrs. Peel [two characters in "The Avengers"] include many who would be the first to complain of sadism in such American series as "The Untouchables" or "Wild, Wild West." Of course, "The Avengers" is viewed by these sophisticates as an elegant send-up. Perhaps they believe that, to paraphrase Burke, violence itself loses half its evil by losing all its grossness.

H. Rap Brown struck to the heart of the matter in his notorious remark (made on camera) that "Violence is as American as cherry pie." The point is that there is nothing specifically American about cherry pie, although the United States probably leads the world in the production and consumption of this delicacy. So with violence. American culture has no monopoly in the sanction of domestic (not to mention international) aggressiveness, but it also has no serious rival among the advanced nations of the world. In a country which is engaged in a savage and highly visible war and where some sixty-five hundred citizens were murdered last year, it is asking too much to expect that popular art should be irradiated with the values of brotherhood, sweetness, and light. One can sympathize with the motives that prompt Dr. Frederic Wertham's crusade against media violence, and share his dismay at the findings of a survey which showed that in one week on the television channels of a large American city, there were 7,887 acts and 1,087 threats of violence, without agreeing with him that to attack these symptoms is the best way to cure the communal disease. In any case, the most casual and fragmented (and therefore the most obscene) images of violence are to be found these days on the news shows, and one assumes that Dr. Wertham is not trying to clean *them* up.

Calculated Exploitation?

If they prove anything, these horrific statistics indicate that the cult of violence is based upon something far more serious than the desire of a few cynical men to get rich by pandering to base appetites. Video mayhem on that scale could not be the product of rational calculation. Something much more sinister and atavistic must be involved. The tragic truth seems to be that the greatest popular myth of twentieth century America has become not merely irrelevant (in which case it would cease to be popular and fade away) but lethal and neurotic. The western and its urban counterpart, the crime thriller, incarnate virtually all the most dangerous tendencies of man in twentieth century mass society: contempt for legal authority or due process, the glorification of alienation, the resort to individual violence, and racist attitudes toward Indians, Mexicans, or urban minority groups. If it were practical, there might be something to be said for banning these genres from the television screen.

Since it is not practical, and since getting rid of the programs would not get rid of the public attitudes to which they appeal, the enlightened solution is to use the myth creatively in the service of a less antisocial vision. This, I take it, was the fumbling and half-conscious intention of a movie which has been quite savagely attacked for its exploitation of violence, *Bonnie and Clyde*. This picture beautifully combined a nostalgic, pastoral evocation of smalltown life in the South and Midwest during the thirties with a realistic emphasis upon its physical and emotional poverty. It explained why this environment produced minor desperadoes like Clyde Barrow and why they became heroic figures to many an ostensibly respectable American. Though the audience was en-

couraged to identify with the almost innocent euphoria of
Bonnie and Clyde at the start of their criminal career ("We
rob banks!"), the sinister consequences of their violence, both
for their victims and themselves, is made increasingly explicit
until its climax in the gruesome ambush which ends their
lives and the picture. Our ambiguous feelings about the protagonists seem to me to be exactly appropriate to the dramatic situation. Was it luck or genius that inspired the
choice of a story with this particular setting in space and
time? Bonnie and Clyde are heirs to the territory and much
of the glamorous tradition of the western outlaw, but their
lifestyle and their technological sophistication resemble
those of the urban gangster; at the same time, they are not,
like the cowboy, cut off from us by temporal remoteness or,
like the mob leader, by penthouse affluence. Hence, the astonishing mythic force of the picture. Of course, since this
is a commercial product of the Hollywood studios, *Bonnie
and Clyde* does not consistently maintain its own highest
standards: in particular the theme of Clyde's impotence is
handled with all the subtlety and insight of a sophomore
psychologist.

To Dr. Wertham, of course, *Bonnie and Clyde* is no more
than the sum total of its violent episodes, but I hope that I
have indicated some of the ways in which the film provides
a model that television producers might emulate—if only they
were allowed to think in terms of worthier aims than a top-
ten rating. In any case, the statistical approach to media
violence can be very misleading: how can we compare the
enemies of CONTROL dying like flies at the end of a "Get
Smart" episode with a single savage beating in (say) "Gun-
smoke," the camera up close from below and focused on the
sadistic twitch at the corners of the assailant's mouth? It is
well known that a violent argument between husband and
wife in a domestic drama can be more disturbing to juvenile
viewers than half a dozen shootings in a typical western
which, though exciting, does not dramatize a situation with
which they closely identify.

Problem of Verbal Confrontations

That this generalization applies to adults as well as to children is suggested by the fact that the most disturbing programs dealing with the racial conflicts of the past few months have not been those which showed cities burning, police and rioters battling, or even the distended bellies of starving southern children—dreadful though these spectacles were. The greatest and most salutary shocks to white complacency and self-confidence were applied by purely verbal confrontations between leaders of the black and white communities. One of these was staged during the inaugural program of the Public Broadcasting Laboratory, but I was not able to see it. However, I was an astonished witness of "Civil Rights—What Next?" (NET [National Educational Television], April [1968]. Producer: R. D. Squier) in which three angry blacks in a New York studio overwhelmed three rather feeble and inadequate whites in Washington with an eloquent torrent of argument and invective. While Floyd McKissick of CORE [Congress of Racial Equality], James Foreman of SNCC [Student Nonviolent Coordinating Committee], and Hosea Williams of SCLC [Southern Christian Leadership Conference] kept pouring it on, the unfortunate Washingtonians seemed incapable of reply. They tried to talk against the flow of verbiage, but had trouble concentrating while the sound from New York kept dinning into their earpieces at a volume quite loud enough to be audible to viewers. In desperation, audio from New York was cut off for a few minutes to give the whites a chance to blurt out a few lame words. Then back to New York where it became immediately apparent that the black rhetoric had continued unabated all through this little hiatus.

At the end, the hapless moderator concluded that "to expose racial problems in this country is to exacerbate them." One saw what he meant, even while disagreeing.

Since NET programs have only recently become visible in Montreal, and this was one of the earliest I was able to see, I at first attributed the lack of control over this debate to a low budget and inadequate technical facilities. However, something rather similar happened on a commercial network program, "Newark—the Anatomy of a Riot" (ABC, July [1968]. Producer: Ernest Pendrell), in the series "Time for Americans." Here a number of citizens, black and white, demonstrated that Newark is a long way from either agreeing on the causes of last year's outbreak or taking the kind of action that will prevent a recurrence. The babble of bitter talk between white merchants and black community leaders made it painfully clear that what one participant called the "tragic dance" of hate and suspicion will not soon be ended in Newark. Other programs in the same six-part series were equally depressing: "Bias and the Mass Media" featured two hour-long discussions. On the first, Harry Belafonte, Lena Horne, Larry Neal, and Dr. Alvin Poussaint delivered a choric denunciation of white-owned media, concluding that they "will not permit the people to understand." There was such unanimity and so little direction or discipline to the discussion that the program became boring. So did its successor the following week, though for different reasons. Here, the impassioned common sense of Norman Cousins of the *Saturday Review* and Edward P. Morgan of NET shone fitfully amidst the ponderous evasiveness of a gaggle of top media brass.

"Prejudice and the Police" was at once more dramatic and more sinister. This program confronted nine members of the Houston police force with an equal number of citizens, mostly black or Mexican. It was one of a number of similar group sessions organized by the city to enable police and public to engage in face-to-face discussion. The chief obstacle to dialogue was the truculent defensiveness of the police. To a man, they refused to admit that there was substance to complaints of violence and lack of respect put forward, with great moderation and charity, by the colored citizens. Only the example of the endlessly patient group leaders added an element of hope to this ugly little vignette of life in Texas.

With their admirably American faith in the sure triumph of reason and goodwill if people can be made to level with each other, they carried on with discussion, psychodrama, and role reversal as though oblivious to the policemen's sullen self-righteousness.

Whatever may happen on the city streets, this [1968] is certainly proving to be a long hot summer for this kind of confrontation on television. As though responding to the urging of some unseen prompter, all the networks have scheduled a total of about two dozen specials devoted wholly or in part to the racial crisis. Cynics may observe that summer is a period of low ratings and panel shows are cheap to produce; optimists might retort that prime time is prime time, and low budgets may have unintended advantages. The underproduced rawness and untidiness of human relations on the programs I have been describing is much closer to the reality of black-white interaction than a more disciplined format would suggest.

But even this kind of program involves its own characteristic form of distortion. Black audiences may watch (if they do) for the pleasure of seeing the white establishment being outtalked or unmasked, but they do not learn anything about their situation that they did not know before. It is the white audience that is being enlightened and informed. Blackness is not taken for granted as part of the kaleidoscopic variety of American life, but exposed as a problem, a threat to the status quo. In other words, these well-intentioned and wholly admirable programs cannot avoid defining normality (and hence, by extension, "reality") in terms of whiteness.

Two Possible Alternatives

So far as the media are concerned, there are two possible cures for this intolerable social disease. Both are being tried this year, in timid, experimental doses, though they are ultimately incompatible with one another. Either of them, if seriously attempted, would involve a more radical reform of current practice than anything now being dreamed of at NBC or CBS.

The first alternative is to make darkness visible throughout the media. I well remember my surprise at the racial variety in the streets of New York, upon my first visit three years ago: Hollywood's version of American reality tended to suppress that little detail. Things have improved somewhat since then, and there are apparently plans afoot to enrich the racial mix on both programs and commercials this autumn. However, there are limits to what can be accomplished along these lines. So long as Bill Cosby cannot lay a hand on a white chick in "I Spy," his visibility tends to emphasize his inferior status. Furthermore, television's view of life tends to be not merely lilywhite, but even more fervently bourgeois. One can imagine network executives coming to accept a kind of *café-au-lait* consciousness, but not the matriarchal, proletarian values of the great black ghettos.

A more promising alternative would be to establish black-owned and operated outlets in large cities. This is a project that might interest the Ford Foundation, which has shown a willingness to support relatively radical experiments in the field of public communications. However, it is doubtful whether the Foundation would be prepared to tolerate the inevitably heterodox political, social, and sexual orientation of such stations. Local white communities would presumably be even less sympathetic. Yet this kind of facility is a necessity for any minority which wishes to maintain its identity in the modern world.

In the meantime, a few small experiments in programing by and for black people are under way. National Educational Television leads the way with two regular series. "History of the Negro People" is a series of half-hour programs devoted to uncovering the heritage, African and American, of black culture; and "Black Journal" (editor: Louis Potter) is a moderately lively hour-long weekly magazine-type show which seems to be hitting its stride after an understandably shaky start.

"Of Black America" (CBS), a rather lavish series of documentaries and panel discussions, was not produced by or exclusively for black viewers but it has managed so far to avoid acquiring too whitish an aura. The first program, "Black History: Lost, Strayed, or Stolen" (Producers: Andrew Rooney and Perry Wolf), narrated by Bill Cosby, was a masterpiece of research, editing, and cool, hip commentary. The use of old and new film clips to illustrate prejudice and stereotypes was both hilarious and appalling. "The Black Soldier" (Producer: Peter Poor), though limited by its thirty-minute format, used old drawings and still photos very effectively, the camera zooming in to single out the "invisible" black faces among the armies of a dozen American wars. Other programs in the series . . . have not been quite so successful. Nevertheless, "Of Black America" at its best demonstrates what superlative resources of intelligence, public spirit, and style CBS News can marshal when it wants to and is given the chance. What a pity the parent organization displays so few of the same qualities. But then intelligence, public spirit, and style have limited value to a business whose main purpose is to sell soap, cars, and cheese.

THE IMPACT ACCORDING TO McLUHAN [4]

Marshall McLuhan, one of the most acclaimed, most controversial and certainly most talked-about of contemporary intellectuals, displays little of the stuff of which prophets are made. Tall, thin, middle-aged and graying, he has a face of such meager individual character that it is difficult to remember exactly what he looks like; different photographs of him rarely seem to capture the same man.

[4] From "Understanding McLuhan (in Part)," article by Richard Kostelanetz, critic and cultural historian, author of *The Theatre of Mixed Means*. New York *Times Magazine*. p 18-19+. Ja. 29, '67. © by The New York Times Company. Reprinted by permission. A revised and expanded version of the text is to appear in the author's forthcoming *Master Minds* (Macmillan).

By trade, he is a professor of English at . . . the University of Toronto. Except for a seminar called "Communication," the courses he teaches are the standard fare of Mod. Lit. and Crit., and around the university he has hardly been a celebrity. One young woman now in Toronto publishing remembers that, a decade ago, "McLuhan was a bit of a campus joke." Even now, only a few of his graduate students seem familiar with his studies of the impact of communications media on civilization—those famous books that have excited so many outside Toronto.

McLuhan's two major works, *The Gutenberg Galaxy* (1962) and *Understanding Media* (1964), have won an astonishing variety of admirers. General Electric, IBM and Bell Telephone have all had him address their top executives; so have the publishers of America's largest magazines. The composer John Cage made a pilgrimage to Toronto especially to pay homage to McLuhan, and the critic Susan Sontag has praised his "grasp on the texture of contemporary reality."

He has a number of eminent and vehement detractors, too. The critic Dwight Macdonald calls McLuhan's books "impure nonsense, nonsense adulterated by sense." Leslie Fiedler wrote in *Partisan Review*: "Marshall McLuhan . . . continually risks sounding like the body-fluids man in *Doctor Strangelove*." . . .

What makes McLuhan's success so surprising is that his books contain little of the slick style of which popular sociology is usually made. As anyone who opens the covers immediately discovers, *Media* and *Galaxy* are horrendously difficult to read—clumsily written, frequently contradictory, oddly organized, and overlaid with their author's singular jargon. Try this sample from *Understanding Media*. Good luck.

The movie, by sheer speeding up the mechanical, carried us from the world of sequence and connections into the world of creative configuration and structure. The message of the movie medium is that of transition from lineal connections to configurations. It is the transition that produced the now quite correct observation: "If it works, it's obsolete." When electric speed further takes over from mechanical movie sequences, then the lines of force in structures and in media become loud and clear. We return to the inclusive form of the icon.

Exponent of "Technological Determinism"

Everything McLuhan writes is originally dictated, either to his secretary or to his wife, and he is reluctant to rewrite, because, he explains, "I tend to add, and the whole thing gets out of hand." Moreover, some of his insights are so original that they evade immediate understanding; other paragraphs may forever evade explication. "Most clear writing is a sign that there is no exploration going on," he rationalizes. "Clear prose indicates the absence of thought."

The basic themes in these books seem difficult at first, because the concepts are as unfamiliar as the language, but on second (or maybe third) thought, the ideas are really quite simple. In looking at history, McLuhan espouses a position one can only call "technological determinism." That is, whereas Karl Marx, an economic determinist, believed that the economic organization of a society shapes every important aspect of its life, McLuhan believes that crucial technological inventions are the primary influence. McLuhan admires the work of the historian Lynn White, Jr., who wrote in *Medieval Technology and Social Change* (1962) that the three inventions of the stirrup, the nailed horseshoe and the horse collar created the Middle Ages. With the stirrup, a soldier could carry armor and mount a charger; and the horseshoe and the harness brought more efficient tilling of the land, which shaped the feudal system of agriculture, which, in turn, paid for the soldier's armor.

Pursuing this insight into technology's importance, McLuhan develops a narrower scheme. He maintains that a major shift in society's predominant technology of communication is the crucially determining force behind social changes, initiating great transformations not only in social organization but human sensibilities. He suggests in *The Gutenberg*

Galaxy that the invention of movable type shaped the culture of Western Europe from 1500 to 1900. The mass production of printed materials encouraged nationalism by allowing more rapid and wider spread of information than permitted by hand-written messages. The linear forms of print influenced music to repudiate the structure of repetition, as in Gregorian chants, for that of linear development, as in a symphony. Also, print reshaped the sensibility of Western man, for whereas he once saw experience as individual segments, as a collection of separate entities, man in the Renaissance saw life as he saw print—as a continuity, often with causal relationships. Print even made Protestantism possible, because the printed book, by enabling people to think alone, encouraged individual revelation. Finally: "All forms of mechanization emerge from movable type, for type is the prototype of all machines."

In *Understanding Media,* McLuhan suggests that electric modes of communication—telegraph, radio, television, movies, telephones, computers—are similarly reshaping civilization in the twentieth century. Whereas print-age man saw one thing at a time in consecutive sequence—like a line of type—contemporary man experiences numerous forces of communication simultaneously, often through more than one of his senses. Contrast, for example, the way most of us read a book with how we look at a newspaper. With the latter, we do not start one story, read it through and then start another. Rather, we shift our eyes across the pages, assimilating a discontinuous collection of headlines, subheadlines, lead paragraphs, photographs and advertisements. "People don't actually read newspapers," McLuhan says; "they get into them every morning like a hot bath."

A Global Village

Moreover, the electronic media initiate sweeping changes in the distribution of sensory awareness—in what McLuhan calls the "sensory ratios." A painting or a book strikes us through only one sense, the visual; motion pictures and television hit us not only visually but also aurally. The new media envelop us, asking us to participate. McLuhan believes that such a multisensory existence is bringing a return to the primitive man's emphasis upon the sense of touch, which he considers the primary sense, "because it consists of a meeting of the senses." Politically, he sees the new media as transforming the world into "a global village," where all ends of the earth are in immediate touch with one another, as well as fostering a "retribalization" of human life. "Any highway eatery with its TV set, newspaper and magazine," he writes, "is as cosmopolitan as New York or Paris."

In his over-all view of human history, McLuhan posits four great stages: (1) totally oral, preliterate tribalism; (2) the codification by script that arose after Homer in ancient Greece and lasted 2,000 years; (3) the age of print, roughly from 1500 to 1900; (4) the age of electronic media, from before 1900 to the present. Underpinning this classification is his thesis that "societies have been shaped more by the nature of the media by which men communicate than by the content of the communication."

This approach to the question of human development, it should be pointed out, is not wholly original. McLuhan is modest enough to note his indebtedness to such works as E. H. Gombrich's *Art and Illusion* (1960), H. A. Innis's *The Bias of Communication* (1951, recently reissued with an introduction by McLuhan), Siegfried Giedion's *Mechanization Takes Command* (1948), H. J. Chaytor's *From Script to Print* (1945) and Lewis Mumford's *Technics and Civilization* (1934).

McLuhan's discussions of the individual media move far beyond the trade talk of communications professionals (he dismisses General David Sarnoff, the board chairman of RCA, as "the voice of the current somnambulism"). Serious critics of the new media usually complain about their content, arguing, for example, that if television had more intelligent treatments of more intelligent subjects, its contribution to culture would be greater. McLuhan proposes that, instead, we think more about the character and form of the new media. His most famous epigram—"The medium is the message"—means several things.

The phrase first suggests that each medium develops an audience of people whose love for that medium is greater than their concern for its content. That is, the TV medium itself becomes the prime interest in watching television; just as some people like to read for the joy of experiencing print, and more find great pleasure in talking to just anybody on the telephone, so others like television for the mixture of kinetic screen and relevant sound. Second, the "message" of a medium is the impact of its forms upon society. The "message" of print was all the aspects of Western culture that print influenced. "The message of the movie medium is that of transition from linear connections to configurations." Third, the aphorism suggests that the medium itself—its form—shapes its limitations and possibilities for the communication of content. One medium is better than another at evoking a certain experience. American football, for example, is better on television than on radio or in a newspaper column; a bad football game on television is more interesting than a great game on radio. Most congressional hearings, in contrast, are less boring in the newspaper than on television. Each medium seems to possess a hidden taste mechanism that encourages some styles and rejects others.

To define this mechanism, McLuhan has devised the categories of "hot" and "cool" to describe simultaneously the composition of a communications instrument or a communicated experience, and its interaction with human attention. A "hot" medium or experience has a "high definition" or a highly individualized character as well as a considerable amount of detailed information. "Cool" is "low" in definition and information; it requires that the audience participate to complete the experience. McLuhan's own examples clarify the distinction: "A cartoon is 'low' definition, simply because very little visual information is provided." Radio is usually a hot medium; print, photography, film and paintings essentially are hot media. "Any hot medium allows of less participating than a cool one, as a lecture makes for less participation than a seminar, and a book for less than a dialogue."

The terms "hot" and "cool" he also applies to experiences and people, and, pursuing his distinction, he suggests that while a hot medium favors a performer of a strongly individualized presence, cool media prefer more nonchalant, "cooler" people. Whereas the radio medium needs a voice of a highly idiosyncratic quality that is instantly recognizable—think of Westbrook Van Voorhees, Jean Shepherd, Fanny Brice—television favors people of a definition so low they appear positively ordinary. With these terms, one can then explain all sorts of phenomena previously inscrutable—such as why bland personalities (Ed Sullivan, Jack Paar) are so successful on television.

It was no accident that Senator McCarthy lasted such a very short time when he switched to TV [McLuhan says]. TV is a cool medium. It rejects hot figures and hot issues and people from the hot press media. Had TV occurred on a large scale during Hitler's reign he would have vanished quickly.

As for the 1960 presidential debates, McLuhan explains that whereas Richard Nixon, essentially a hot person, was superior on radio, John F. Kennedy was the more appealing television personality. (It follows that someone with as low a definition as Dwight Eisenhower would have been more successful than either.)

Brilliant Insight, Wacky Nonsense

The ideas are not as neatly presented as this summary might suggest, for McLuhan believes more in probing and exploring—"making discoveries"—than in offering final definitions. For this reason, he will rarely defend any of his statements as absolute truths, although he will explain how he developed them. Some perceptions are considerably more tenable than others—indeed, some are patently ridiculous—and all his original propositions are arguable, so his books require the participation of each reader to separate what is wheat to him from the chaff. In McLuhanese, they offer a cool experience in a hot medium.

A typical reader's scorecard for *Media* might show that about one half is brilliant insight; one fourth, suggestive hypotheses; one fourth, nonsense. Given the book's purpose and originality, these are hardly bad percentages. "If a few details here and there are wacky," McLuhan says, "it doesn't matter a hoot."

McLuhan eschews the traditional English professor's expository style—introduction, development, elaboration and conclusion. Instead, his books imitate the segmented structure of the modern media. He makes a series of direct statements. None of them becomes a thesis but all of them approach the same phenomenon from different angles. This means that one should not necessarily read his books from start to finish—the archaic habit of print-man.

The real introduction to *The Gutenberg Galaxy* is the final chapter, called "The Galaxy Reconfigured"; even McLuhan advises his readers to start there. With *Media,* the introduction and the first two chapters form the best starting point; thereafter, the reader is pretty much free to wander as he wishes. "One can stop anywhere after the first few sentences and have the full message, if one is prepared to 'dig' it," McLuhan once wrote of non-Western scriptural literature; the remark is applicable to his own books.

Similarly, McLuhan does not believe that his works have only one final meaning. "My book," he says, "is not a package but part of the dialogue, part of the conversation." (Indeed, he evaluates other books less by how definitively they treat their subject—the academic standard—than by how much thought they stimulate. Thus, a book may be wrong but still great. By his own standards, *Media* is, needless to say, a masterpiece.)

Underlying McLuhan's ideas is the question of whether technology is beneficial to man. Thinkers such as the British critic F. R. Leavis have argued, on the one hand, that technology stifles the blood of life by dehumanizing the spirit and cutting existence off from nature; more materialist thinkers, on the other hand, defend the machine for easing man's burdens. McLuhan recognizes that electronic modes of communication represent, in the subtitle of *Media,* "extensions of man." Whereas the telephone is an extension of the ear (and voice), so television extends our eyes and ears. That is, our eyes and ears attended John Kennedy's funeral, but our bodies stayed at home. As extensions, the new media offer both possibility and threat, for while they lengthen man's reach into his existence, they can also extend society's reach into him, for both exploitation and control.

To prevent this latter possibility, McLuhan insists that every man should know as much about the media as possible.

By knowing how technology shapes our environment, we can transcend its absolutely determining power [he says]. Actually, rather than a "technological determinist," it would be more accurate to say, as regards the future, that I am an "organic autonomist." My entire concern is to overcome the determinism that results from the determination of people to ignore what is going on. Far from regarding technological change as inevitable, I insist that if we understand its components we can turn it off any time we choose. Short of turning it off, there are lots of moderate controls conceivable.

In brief, in stressing the importance of knowledge, McLuhan is a humanist.

McLuhan advocates radical changes in education, because he believes that a contemporary man is not fully "literate" if reading is his sole pleasure: "You must be literate in umpteen media to be really 'literate' nowadays." Education, he suggests, should abandon its commitment to print—merely a focusing of the visual sense—to cultivate the "total sensorium" of man—to teach us how to use all five cylinders, rather than only one. "Postliterate does not mean illiterate," writes the Rev. John Culkin, S.J., director of the Communications Center at Fordham [University] and a veteran propagator of McLuhan's ideas about multimedia education. "It rather describes the new social environment within which print will interact with a great variety of communications media.". . .

Conjuring Insights

McLuhan seems pretty much like any other small-city professor until he begins to speak. His lectures and conversation are a singular mixture of original assertions, imaginative comparisons, heady abstractions and fantastically comprehensive generalizations, and no sooner has he stunned his listeners with one extraordinary thought than he hits them with another. His phrases are more oracular than his manner; he makes the most extraordinary statements in the driest media.". . .

In his graduate seminar, he asks: "What is the future of old age?" The students look bewildered. "Why," he replies to his own question, "exploration and discovery." Nearly everything he says *sounds* important. Before long, he has characterized the "Batman" TV show as "simply an exploitation of nostalgia which I predicted years ago." The twenty-five or so students still look befuddled and dazed; hardly anyone talks but McLuhan. "The criminal, like the artist, is a social explorer," he goes on. "Bad news reveals the character of change; good news does not." No one asks him to be more definite, because his talk intimidates his listeners.

He seems enormously opinionated; in fact, he conjures insights. His method demands a memory as prodigious as his curiosity. He often elevates an analogy into a grandiose generalization, and he likes to make his points with puns: "When a thing is current, it creates currency." His critics ridicule him as a communications expert who cannot successfully communicate; but too many of his listeners, say his admirers, suffer from closed minds.

The major incongruity is that a man so intellectually adventurous should lead such a conservative life; the ego-centric and passionately prophetic qualities of his books contrast with the personal modesty and pervasive confidence of a secure Catholic. What explains the paradox is that "Marshall McLuhan," the thinker, is different from "H. M. Mc-Luhan," the man. The one writes books and delivers lectures; the other teaches school, heads a family and lists himself in the phone book. It was probably H. M. who made that often-quoted remark about Marshall's theories: "I don't pretend to understand them. After all, my stuff is very difficult."

And the private H. M. will say this about the technologies his public self has so brilliantly explored:

I wish none of these had ever happened. They impress me as nothing but a disaster. They are for dissatisfied people. Why is man so unhappy he wants to change his world? I would never attempt to improve an environment—my personal preference, I suppose, would be a preliterate milieu, but I want to study change to gain power over it.

His books, he adds, are just "probes"—that is, he does not "believe" in his work as he believes in Catholicism. The latter is faith; the books are just thoughts. "You know the faith differently from the way you 'understand' my books."

When asked why he creates books rather than films, a medium that might be more appropriate to his ideas, McLuhan replies: "Print is the medium I trained myself to handle." So, all the recent acclaim has transformed McLuhan into a bookmaking machine. . . . Perhaps reflecting his own idea that future art will be, like medieval art, corporate in authorship, McLuhan is producing several more books in dialogue with others. With Wilfred Watson, a former student who is now an English professor at the University of Alberta, he is completing a history of stylistic change, "From Cliché to Archetype." With Harley W. Parker, head of design at the Royal Ontario Museum, he has just finished *Through the Vanishing Point: Space in Poetry and Painting* [1968, Harper], a critical and comparative survey of thirty-five pairs of poems and pictures from primitive times to the present.

In tandem with William Jovanovich, the president of Harcourt, Brace and World, McLuhan is writing "The Future of the Book," a study of the impact of xerography, and along with the management consultant Ralph Baldwin he is investigating the future of business in "Report to Management." As if that were not enough, he joined with the book designer Quentin Fiore to compile *The Medium Is the Massage* [1967, Random House], an illustrated introduction to McLuhanism . . .; the two are doing another book on the effect of automation. Finally, McLuhan has contributed an appendix to *McLuhan Hot and Cool* [1967, Dial Press], a collection of critical essays about him. . . .

McLuhan has always been essentially a professor living in an academic community, a father in close touch with his large family and a teacher who also writes and lectures. When some VIP's invited him to New York a year ago, he kept them waiting while he graded papers. Although he does not run away from all the reporters and visitors, he does little to attract publicity. His passion is the dialogue; if the visitor can participate in the conversation, he may be lucky enough, as this writer was, to help McLuhan write (that is, dictate) a chapter of a book.

Most people [McLuhan once remarked] are alive in an earlier time, but you must be alive in our own time. The artist is the man in any field, scientific or humanistic, who grasps the implications of his actions and of new knowledge in his own time. He is the man of integral awareness.

Although his intention was otherwise, McLuhan was describing himself—the specialist in general knowledge. Who would dare surmise what thoughts, what perceptions, what grand schemes he will offer next?

THE McLUHAN CULT [5]

The McLuhan Follies, now playing to full houses in all the "media" and about to open in several new versions, had its first preview when a McGraw-Hill editor working on

[5] From "The McLuhan Follies," by Robert Meister, editor of the *Journal of Existentialism. New Leader.* 49:2O-1. O. 10, '66. Reprinted from *The New Leader* of October 10, 1966. Copyright © 1966 The American Labor Conference on International Affairs, Inc.

Understanding Media "noted in dismay," as recorded by
McLuhan, "that '75 per cent of your material is new. A successful book cannot venture to be more than 10 per cent
new.'" Still and all, the editor went on, "Such a risk seems
quite worth taking at the present time when the stakes are
very high, and the need to understand the effects of the extensions of man becomes more urgent by the hour."

We are in McLuhan's debt for preserving his editor's remark. Beyond its obvious use in pinpointing the sort of men-
tality that dominates today's publishing industry, it serves
the no doubt unintended function of helping to explain the
McLuhan cult with its subordination of logic and substance
to apocalyptic novelty and specious complexity.

That such a cult is flourishing indeed is overpoweringly
obvious. . . . [Formerly] it was restricted to the Madison
Avenue scene, where McLuhan served as an astronomically
priced consultant; but since the *Wunderkind* and the Magic
Elixir are staples thereabouts, no one paid much attention.
Then, largely through the efforts of the Plutarch of the Underground, Tom Wolfe, the input to the public's central
nervous system (McLuhan's most favored image) was ac-
tivated, and before one could say "interiorization of the
technology of the phonetic alphabet," McLuhan became an
important public figure, the center of a sizable cult, and
subject to only uncertain and perplexed criticism. In recent . . . [years] he could be found addressing scholarly meetings, honoring the august pages of the *American Scholar*
with the première of his full name, Herbert Marshall Mc-
Luhan, parrying the exasperated but polite inquiries of TV
interviewers, and causing a foreign participant in the PEN
[Poets, Playwrights, Editors, Essayists and Novelists (International Association)] congress to proclaim after listening
to his address that he hasn't been "shook up" so much since
reading Spengler thirty years ago. . . .

His books can be spotted in the hands of subway and
bus riders and in bookstore windows so regularly (McLuhan
would call this process "the frequency method of visual iden-

tification") that their sales must be counted by the ton. . . .
All in all, McLuhan is easily the best thing to fall into the
lap of the culture brokers since Andy Warhol.

Every cult has a common denominator, and in this case
one finds it clearly defined in the ingenuously prophetic remark of McLuhan's editor: "Seventy-five per cent of your
material is new." . . . An army of McLuhan interpreters have
taken the "newness" for granted, and then applied it for their
own purposes. Phrases such as "what McLuhan calls . . .,"
"as McLuhan puts it," have become a widespread ploy
whereby the writer clobbers the reader into a suspension of
disbelief with a wave of hallowed texts, having previously
hypnotized himself through laziness or innocence with the
flicker of a mysteriously seductive new knowledge. Thus,
even writers who were unable to find McLuhan persuasive
felt impelled not to close the door on him entirely and reserved the possibility that "newness" may lie buried under
complexities. Complexity has always served well as profun-
dity's stand-in, and in McLuhan's case it has finally gained
top billing.

A disinterested investigation into this curious fuss
emerges with a conclusion so unequivocal that even the possibility of reasonable alternatives seems entirely remote.
Briefly stated, an obscure professor of English from the Canadian provinces has succeeded in perpetrating a hoax so
gigantic that it shows every sign of becoming an international intellectual scandal. By inventing what might be
called a method of incisive inarticulateness, he has managed
to rope in a disturbing number of writers, critics and institutions—in short, a sizable segment of the culture brokerage
game—and has persuaded them to believe that he has opened
a new perspective on what he calls "the extensions of man."
Would you believe it, folks? He has them eating out of his
hand, and they flock to his Center for Culture and Technology, a name so artfully or naïvely dichotomous that it is
a dead giveaway.

In saying that a hoax is "perpetrated," the intention or at least the consciousness of the perpetrator is implied, but on this count, if on no other, one is in doubt. Two feasible alternatives are open: (1) McLuhan is a humorist and has plotted one of the best practical jokes of all time; (2) McLuhan means what he says. All that can be said of his motives up to this writing is that verification of the first alternative would be far more beneficial for all of us; read as a humorist, McLuhan is perhaps without peer, whereas taken seriously he is catastrophic.

Blanket condemnations owe the reader documentary support provided in the most systematic manner possible. The way things are with McLuhan—namely, without a semblance of system or context, completely at random—documentation can only be random, though always delightful. Following then are a few selections from the chapter glosses in *The Gutenberg Galaxy*:

King Lear is a working model of the process of denudation by which men translated themselves from a world of roles to a world of jobs.

When technology extends *one* of our senses, a new translation of culture occurs as swiftly as the new technology is interiorized.

The increase of visual stress among the Greeks alienated them from the primitive art that the electronic age now reinvents after interiorizing the 'unified field' of electric all-at-onceness.

Only a fraction of the history of literacy has been typographic.

For the oral man the literal text contains all possible levels of meaning.

Philosophy was as naïve as science in its unconscious acceptance of the assumptions or dynamic of typography.

Heidegger surf-boards along on the electronic wave as triumphantly as Descartes rode the mechanical wave.

It is difficult to quote complete statements from the text of *The Gutenberg Galaxy*, for it contains scarcely a single paragraph in nearly three hundred pages that does not convolute with quotations from other, often dubious, works:

Wrapped in quotations, one might quote, as a beggar would
enfold himself in the purple of emperors. In essence, *Galaxy*
uses the erudition ploy to conceal what one could guardedly
call its thesis, namely, that Gutenberg's invention of type
was the single most influential event in the history of Western man. No comment is needed on McLuhan's wafer-thin
thesis; as for the erudition—the "packaging," he would call
it—it is pungently indiscriminate and it swings.

In *Understanding Media* the number of direct quotations is reduced in favor of complex-ergo-profound phrase
constructions nimbly substituting for reasoned argument.
Epigrammatic postulates take the place of exposition, and
more often than not, heavy-handed and sweaty they are. The
following paragraph is typical:

Just prior to 1914, the Germans had become obsessed with the
menace of "encirclement." Their neighbors had all developed elaborate railway systems that facilitated mobilization of manpower
resources. Encirclement is a highly visual image that had great
novelty for this newly industrialized nation. In the 1930's, by contrast, the German obsession was with *lebensraum*. This is not a
visual concern, at all. It is a claustrophobia, engendered by the
radio implosion and compression of space. . . .

The construction of random "contrasts" is a characteristic device, and so is the personal use of historical events
which are, as in the above citation, charmingly surrealistic.
See the same device applied to a smaller setting:

Persons grouped around a fire or candle for warmth or light are
less able to pursue independent thoughts, or even tasks, than people supplied with electric light.

Incisive inarticulateness, then, is not only method but,
almost by definition, also content. Still, dismissing McLuhan
as a "thinker" and reading him for humor—which is highly
recommended—leaves the far more serious matter of his fol-
lowers. Is one to assume on the weighty basis of this prece-
dent that so many of our intellectuals are too lazy or incom-
petent to see behind wordage or, what is even more
disconcerting, that they are mere careerists, engaged in

"taste-making," sniffing around like truffle-hounds for the next chic movement? Both assumptions—and their combination—seem not only possible but probable and *"la trahison des clercs"* [treason of the intellectuals], proclaimed by Julien Benda some thirty years ago, is upon us once more.

II. CURRENT TRENDS IN THE MASS MEDIA

EDITOR'S INTRODUCTION

Some of us would agree with Bertrand Russell that "progress is moral." But others might opt for the more mundane view which holds that progress is scientific. For the former group, current trends in the mass media may not seem particularly satisfying, but for the latter there are many grounds for encouragement. Much in the way of scientific progress is going on in the mass media today, from the advent of communications satellites to the spread of cable TV.

This section seeks to examine some of the more interesting current trends in mass communications—both scientific and moral—in detail. In the first article an aircraft company executive with special knowledge of communications satellite technology surveys scientific developments in mass communications from the time of Sir Francis Drake. He expresses concern that our capacity for technological change may be outstripping our capacity for social change and adaptation.

The next two articles deal with two important trends in television. In the first of these a former special consultant on urban problems describes the potential of cable television, a system that makes it possible to feed literally hundreds of different programs into TV receivers. He suggests that such a system could soon revolutionize the means of communication within America's ghettos. The second article takes up the role of public—or educational—television, its current faults and its untapped possibilities. Perhaps the most vexing problem facing television in America today is the contrast between the wealth of the commercial stations, which make their play to the mass audience, and the poverty of the public stations, which must assume the role of cultural leadership. But culture, as this article indicates, can be expensive.

In the two articles that follow, the comeback being made by that almost forgotten medium, radio, is described. By following the migration to the suburbs and concentrating upon specialized audiences, such as those in our black ghettos, radio is once again becoming a popular—and profitable—medium.

The last two contributions to this section deal with America's newspapers—the problems facing the mass circulation dailies and the emergence of a so-called underground press that has become a parody of the "respectable" press. In the first of these articles, an assistant editor of the New York *Times* describes what's wrong with American newspapers and offers some prescriptions for renewed health. In the last article an associate editor of the *New Republic* delivers a biting analysis of the underground press.

THE PROMISE OF COMMUNICATIONS SATELLITES [1]

Until quite recently there has been little change, except in degree, in the patterns of communication from the time of Sir Francis Drake. The importance to our habits of Drake and the British Admiralty can hardly be overestimated, for they conceived the pattern which was completed and maintained until the advent of the communication satellite.

In the early development of the British Empire, Drake and his successors established watering stations at every promontory, controlling island, and navigable strait around the world, beginning the effective domination of ocean shipping and communications during the days of the sailing

[1] From "The Future of Communication," a speech delivered at the 22nd annual convention of the Armed Forces Communications and Electronics Association, May 15, 1968, by L. A. Hyland, vice president and general manager, Hughes Aircraft Company. *Vital Speeches of the Day*. 34:605-8. Jl. 15, '68.

craft. As steam displaced sail these same geographical points became coaling stations. With the development of electrical communications these same points were valuable as cable landings and later as wireless stations.

Whatever important control . . . [points were] not occupied by the British came under the influence of other European powers or, to a minor degree, of American interests. Communication between points dominated by different powers generally was conducted through the home capitals, so we find both colonialism and geography as the primary factors in the structure of long-distance communications. The limitations of optical signaling and, later of wire conductivity, controlled short-distance communications.

Two Key Dates: 1570 and 1963

Technological advances slowly crept in and improved and extended, in small increments, the utility of communication within these basic limitations during the four hundred years between the Drake explorations and the first synchronous communication satellite. The important dates then in the history of communication are 1570 and 1963. Why is 1963 important? Why is the year of the launching of the first syncom such a major milestone in the history of communications? . . .

With the advent of the communication satellite . . . , the barriers of geography and the painfully erected structures of bureaucracy by which our communications have been controlled are crumbling.

Let me recite a few examples. First the rate structure. The transoceanic rates for communication via satellite are not based on satellite costs, but are set to protect investments already made in cables and radio transmission. Although the United States has a monopoly on satellite communication because of its booster and spacecraft technology, nevertheless the protective rates are only a temporary umbrella. Other nations, especially those in the Communist world, will com-

bine to utilize boosters of their own and cut under this monopoly with more realistic rates. This is not a threat; it is a
promise if we persist in our present rate practices.

Another example: the cost of establishing communication in the underdeveloped or sparsely settled countries
using conventional land-line or land-radio techniques is pro-
hibitive. But with current satellite technology, newly developed beaming systems and the capability of multiple voice,
television, and information channels, there can be remarkably flexible choices as to area coverage both for one-way
and two-way communication. It is almost a paradox that
those nations without an existing communications plant
may be the first to benefit fully from the new technology by
having a truly modern system made possible by satellites.
That result can flow from the following considerations:

All of you who have been in business know that the
existence of factories, special tooling, established markets,
and ongoing marketing organizations, are a major hindrance
in a change-over otherwise enabled by newer technologies or
changing public demands. It is the responsibility of the established manufacturer or operator to introduce new products in such manner as to minimize the prospect of economic
loss to his customer as well as to himself. This practice slows
down the adoption of new devices or operating modes, particularly where the existing investment is large. No better
example of this fact could be found than in the peculiar way
mankind is moving to grasp the applications that will be
possible as a consequence of communication satellites. There
will be impact not only with respect to the satellite systems
themselves, but also in the changes to other kinds of communications which will be forced by adaptation to the employment of satellites.

It is entirely possible that many of the developing countries will have modern communication systems much sooner,
for example, than the United States because they have little
investment in older systems and hence no problem in the
write-off on existing investments. . . .

Impact of Communication Satellite

Let's review a few familiar facts that will affect the nature of the changes which will take place.

First, although publicly used television is perhaps only twenty-five years old, there are today in this country some 120 million television receivers as against 90 million telephones. And, of course, the number of radio broadcast receivers is far greater than the count of television sets. This means then that the facilities for mass communications far outnumber those for individual communication. I am sure that the ratio between the numbers of mass receivers and of individual terminal handsets will steadily increase from here on out.

Second, both mass and individual communication systems have heretofore been limited by either or both of geographical and national boundaries, but these boundaries are now becoming meaningless from the communications viewpoint.

Third, in the space of five and one half years the channel capacity of synchronous satellites has increased from one two-way channel to the many thousands which will be provided in the forthcoming military tactical communication satellite. Parenthetically, it should be noted that every new venture into expanded communication channels has always been done in the face of questions regarding the prospect of the full use of the new facility, and always the new facility is fully utilized in half the time or less of the most optimistic estimate.

Fourthly, the communications business is one of the great growth businesses in the developed countries with no saturation in sight as the added facilities and services become available. Yet these developed countries account for only a fourth of the world's population. The need for both individual and mass communication media in the developing countries will provide one of the greatest markets of any technological era. It is noteworthy that this need could not be economically satisfied as long as earth-bound, land-lines communication, of whatever source, were the only means by which the necessary services could be made available. With the advent of high capacity satellites having selective area coverage and selective beam widths, the economic cost is reduced to the point where the most remote village could be provided with effective information links, whether individual or en masse. . . .

That we have done as well as we have with the existing administrative, cooperative, and regulatory agencies during the progress of communications to date has been in my opinion largely due to the relatively slow rate of inventions during the four hundred years prior to satellites. With the advent of satellites, however, and their concomitant ground distribution devices, we have a completely new ball game. The opportunities never existed before, the old rules are not appropriate, the administrative agencies obsolescent, and the old operating entities are battling the new realities in a paradoxically vigorous but somnolent passion of yearning for the good old days. The next decade will be interesting.

Broadening Human Understanding

Now I want to depart from this theme and introduce another factor which in my opinion is even more important. In approaching this factor I am going to make the general assumption that the institutional, economic, legal, technical, and political factors for the new era of communications will eventually be solved. That massive achievement, however important and difficult it may be, brings us to the significant issue which for the first time can then be seen in its true dimensions. That issue is understanding. The sole purpose of communications, in whatever field, is to transmit and receive information which can be understood between the parties involved.

The technological limitations on communications prior to radio broadcasting kept information exchange to relatively simple items which could be understood by both parties.

These were items such as prices and other easily definable commercial matters, administrative documents, and letters on family or social affairs.

In these cases, conditioning of the minds of the parties involved had either taken place beforehand, or the subject was easily defined in common terms. Where more complex or unknown elements entered into the situation the common practice was to transport one party to the other for face-to-face communication.

Radio broadcasts added a new dimension to the problem of understanding. The number of people listening was vastly increased but the breadth of the language and the contents of the material broadcast had to be limited by the common denominator of audience understanding. The material of the programs therefore became limited to comedy, light drama, crude violence, music, and news—all tightly edited for widest appeal. The advent of television, first black and white and then color, added to the interest of broadcast information without much improvement of understanding. At least television requires attention even though the program content may be no better. It is, by the way, interesting that broadcasting without pictures is the favorite medium for propagandists and charlatans, whereas in television the stage setting and make-up are as important as the material itself.

I am making these remarks from the standpoint of an American living in an environment of education, culture and language that is as well informed as any national group of people in the world. Yet the understanding of this fortunate group is so limited that the broadcast material is largely aimed at the level of understanding of a twelve-year-old. In Los Angeles we have eleven television channels on the air. Only one of these regularly offers seriously adult programing. We have some fifty radio stations locally, and only two of them are focused upon the mature audience. We do have educational programs—before 7:00 o'clock in the morning. Once in a while we have a Churchillian speaker who can reach both the twelve-year-old and the mature individual, but this level of understanding is the best we have been able to do in the United States.

Technology Outstrips Man's Capacity

Now picture in your mind what we shall be able to do on a continent-wide, or world-wide basis with no common language, with millions who have never been out of the immediate area they were born in, with primitive cultures and little experience with a society of more than a few hundred people. Technology has made it possible for us to reach these people. With what do we reach them? What is the program content? Will it be reduced to the six-year-old level or should we follow the alternative and attempt to determine the means by which understanding can be conveyed through the application of the scientific method? Our technology has run away from the ability to communicate understanding. Anthropologists have repeatedly assured us there is no difference between the races in brain capacity and ability to learn. The differences which do exist at maturity are the consequences of environment, education, and superstition. The task then is *not* one of permanently degrading the programs to an a priori level of understanding, but of how to *improve* the understanding of the audience. Here there is both challenge and magnificent opportunity.

Consider a few examples. In our neighboring country, Mexico, there are villages in which the national language, Spanish, is not spoken. The people have been passed up by the general national progress—farming, health, and nutrition practices have not improved for centuries. The Mexican government desires to reach these people and draw them into the mainstream of the national life. For this purpose instructional television giving language lessons in the local dialect, instruction in animal husbandry, the care of plots of crop lands, in birth control, in how to make a piece of simple furniture—these services could easily be provided by satellite

link and at very low cost per head if the system deployment
is sufficiently widespread.

The same problem recurs in nation after nation—India,
Pakistan, Brazil, Ecuador—where concerned governments desire to initiate appropriate action programs.

There is more to the solution than simply putting up a
small receiver terminal and a display [TV] tube. One of my
staff people recently witnessed, in Spain, a showing in a remote village of a simple training film on the care of chickens
for local food production. There was a near riot during the
showing as a peasant overturned the screen in an effort to
capture the chickens being pictured on it. He could not
comprehend how the chicken could be seen without being
present in the flesh. He had no understanding. . . .

The changes that have come to pass, for those in the developed nations, are improvements in factual knowledge,
health, nutrition, and in physical facilities. Nothing has been
done about human mutual understanding. The best that can
be said for the governing sector, the opinion makers—and I
must include myself in this indictment—is that they adapted
the age-old principles of control, or influence, to the increasing numbers in national units. However, we seem to
have reached an upper limit to which this adaptation can
take place as evidenced by increased unrest around the world.
It seems to me we can compare the psychological problems
to the medical problems. Humanity did not get very far so
long as medicine was practiced by witch doctors and superstition. Progress commenced with the application of science
to the healing arts and I submit that progress in understanding can be made only by the application of science.

As a matter of fact our progress in technology has only
recently arrived at the point where it can be of use in the
humanities. The jobs that we have done in technology so
far are the easy jobs. . . .

The big job is ahead of us. It is the mission of the engineer to participate and help in bringing about an *under-*

standing of *understanding,* just as it has been the mission of technology to help improve health. . . .

A current example . . . is the President's task force on communications policy which is composed of fifteen members, only two of whom have any technical background. Of these two only one is a communicator. Admitting the vital need for participation by legal, political, and diplomatic experts, it is equally necessary for a substantial number of technologists to be represented on such a committee to elucidate, project, interpose, and judge on the facts relating to the future of communications, and to have a vote in the policy determinations. The facts relating to the achievement of understanding and to the evolution of the great potential of communications technology are not self-evident to the technically unprepared, however sophisticated they otherwise may be. It is not enough for a policy organism merely to consult with technologists. The engineer must be an integral and equivalent part of the decision-making process. In these days of rapid technical change it is difficult even for an expert to keep up with progress and develop that judgment which comes from a lifetime of experience in his field.

In our industry, we have what is called Murphy's law which states that: "In the absence of sure knowledge any choice is bound to be wrong." Therefore, I submit that the time has arrived for the development of knowledge so that we may ultimately bring understanding to the peoples who are making use of the communications achievements now made possible.

THE POTENTIAL OF CABLE TV [2]

Over the past twenty years there has been developed an impressive technological capacity to transmit images and accompanying sound instantaneously and over large dis-

[2] From "Toward a Modest Experiment in Cable Television," by Stephen White, writer on developments in communications, formerly special consultant on urban problems for the Educational Development Center. *Public Interest.* p 52-66. Summer '68. © 1968 by National Affairs, Inc. Reprinted by permission.

tances. Picture definition is surprisingly sharp, and full color transmission is now conventional. The technology is capable also of high fidelity sound, although in practice sound quality at the receiver is usually low. The technology extends also to systems in which image and sound can be stored indefinitely and retrieved at will.

What has been given in the paragraph above is a concise description of an existing communications system. As everyone must be aware, that system is known as television. At the very moment that the name is written or spoken, however, the nature of the system under consideration becomes obscured, for if television (with a small *t*) is a technology, Television (with a capital *T*) is something far more: it is a vast and a complex social institution erected upon that technology. It is extremely difficult to separate the institution and the technology, but it is also crucial that we make a clear differentiation between the two.

What is called to mind by the word *Television* is far more than the box in the corner of the room, or even the complex of condensers, resistors, vacuum tubes, transmitting antenna, relay towers, cameras, and all the rest that combine to create a picture on the tube and an appropriate sound in the speaker. For most citizens of the United States, this is likely to appear the least significant aspect of Television. The reality called up by the word is embodied in the three stations which, in most large cities, carry the current programs prepared and produced at the behest of the three major networks, and those programs themselves. In larger cities, the meaning of the word is extended to include one or more independent commercial stations and perhaps an educational station, and the programs that they too transmit.

These three components of Television—technology, station, and program—have become so intimately associated within the single word that it requires an effort of will, so far as most people are concerned, to examine any one of the three independent of the other two. Unless that effort is

made, it is quite difficult to conceive of the technology operating without the preparation of elaborate and costly programs, selected and organized by individual stations or by
networks operating in behalf of clusters of stations. Television, in this country at least, has never taken any other
form, and even in other countries the differences are minor.

None of this is an accident. The shape of Television in
every country has been determined by the technology itself,
which was the same for all countries, and to a lesser extent by
the social environment in which the technology developed.

The Natural Laws of Television

Television was an inevitable consequence of the discovery that electromagnetic waves could be generated cheaply
and efficiently, could be readily modulated to carry signals,
radiated freely through space, and were readily intercepted
by suitable equipment to deliver on command the signals
that they carried. All of this constituted a communications
system of incredible flexibility and economy. At a cost so
small as to be almost negligible, a message could be sent to
every person within the ample reach of the transmitting
equipment. Initially, the discovery was applied to the transmission of sound only, but from the earliest days of the technology it was apparent that the transmission of both sound
and picture would inevitably follow.

The economy of such a communications system was immediately apparent. The great power of the system was apparent as well. Communication can be conducted in many
ways—by the printed word, by the spoken word, by the still
picture and the moving picture, by gesture, mannerism, tone
of voice, by diagram and animation. Television alone is able
to combine all of these and to deliver the entire bundle of
information in a single moment to thousands or to millions
of receivers. Thus, in potency as well as in economy, television constituted a communications system immeasurably
in advance of anything that had previously existed.

There was, however, a price for all this, and it lay in the laws of nature. One set of laws stipulated that in order to transmit the tremendous amount of information carried by a television signal, a large portion of the electromagnetic spectrum was necessary for each such signal. Another set of laws limited the portion of the electromagnetic spectrum that was suitable for television transmission. A third set of laws, governing interference between electromagnetic waves at or near the same wavelength, prescribed separations among stations, both geographic and with respect to the electromagnetic spectrum. The three sets of laws, taken together, meant that the maximum number of television signals that could be transmitted from any one locality was in theory seven, but that in practice most localities would be limited to two or three if other localities were to have their fair share.

Television, accordingly, came into being as a commodity that was scarce by definition. Like any commodity that is both scarce and in demand, it came at once under pressures which in the end determined the shape of the institution, Television, that grew up around the technology, television.

Television as a Scarce Resource

In the first place, it appeared inescapable that the impressive new system of communications should serve society as a whole, and could not appropriately be reserved for the purposes of the few. Given the scarcity of television stations, this meant that each such station was obliged to serve a large number of people. In Television terms, this meant at once the imposition of some kind of organization upon the choice of signal to be transmitted: it was necessary to determine what would be transmitted on the basis of some kind of principle that would maximize the number of persons who believed themselves to be served by the system.

This appears so natural that it is necessary to point out how unusual, within the field of communications, it actually is. There is, for example, no comparable imperative within the field of publishing. In principle, anyone may publish and may direct his efforts toward any audience he pleases. *Life* seeks to enlist as reader every literate citizen of the United States; at the same time there are professional journals intended for only a few hundred, and elaborate privately printed publications for a few dozen. There is, in fact, no central regulation within publishing: instead there is the free self-regulation of many thousands of individual wills.

Reinforcing this constraint was another which emerged out of the decision to permit the commercial use of television in the United States (although initially not in other countries). The power of television to persuade is enormous. It is, beyond any comparison, the most effective medium for large-scale advertising that has ever been developed. And simply because of this, the financial returns from a small increment of audience are worth almost any investment that the advertiser can reasonably pour into the medium.

With three stations in a community, an advertiser on any one could reasonably expect one third the audience as his share. If, however, by extraordinary efforts that 33 per cent could be increased to 50 per cent or 75 per cent, his return might be tremendously augmented. There are, of course, economic limits to the process, but by and large there are great incentives for the advertiser, and for the network in behalf of the advertiser, to add to the popularity of their programs even at substantial cost. Hence the inevitable increase in the elaborateness with which programs are prepared, and in the fees paid popular or highly persuasive entertainers and salesmen. Hence, also, for easily comprehended reasons, the unwillingness to experiment with new or novel programs, for the risk that lies in failure is as impressive in its own way as the reward that lies in success.

Out of all this has come the shape of the system known as Television. Its principal components, once again, are three:

1. The technology. It has changed considerably since the system came into being, but the basic technology that is now

utilized is, in its important aspects, the technology with which the system was initially endowed.

2. The stations. The decision as to what goes on the air is made either at the individual station, or by networks in behalf of individual stations, in accordance with the encompassing criterion of popularity.

3. The programs. With few exceptions (of which the most important is the local sports program), these are created almost entirely by networks, or in behalf of networks, or by film studios, or are drawn from the backlog of popular productions created earlier by film studios for theatrical exhibition. (Independent stations depend largely upon reruns of network programs.) All programing is highly elaborate: television almost never carries a simple communication. There are some interesting exceptions, and for the sake of stressing, in this place, the degree to which most programs have undergone a high degree of elaboration one such exception might be cited here: in areas where community antenna services have been established, a channel is sometimes given over to the continuous transmission of pictures of a clock face, a thermometer, an anemometer and a humidity indicator, accompanied by unobtrusive phonograph music; another channel may transmit hour after hour a picture of a teletypewriter upon which the latest news is endlessly displayed and redisplayed. Needless to say, in view of what has already been pointed out, no conventional station transmits any program as bare as these....

Television Stations or Channels of Communication?

The technology of television, as described above, was such that Television was able to establish itself by means of a kind of bootstrap operation. Without excessive capital outlays, organizations operating radio transmitters were able to put on the air a television signal even before there were enough television sets to provide a respectable audience. The existence of that signal encouraged householders to invest in sets; that investment, spread more or less evenly over the entire population, is the largest single form of capital investment in television. It can therefore be said that it was the economy of the signal which led, at the outset, to the establishment of Television within the society with such great speed.

From the beginning there was an alternative technology which could have provided, although at great initial cost, a television service superior in every important respect to open-circuit broadcasting. The signal that is carried through open space by electromagnetic radiation can also be carried within the confines of a coaxial cable. Transmission by coaxial cable is free from interference emanating out of electrical systems outside the system, and is equally free from "ghosts" caused by reflection from buildings and topographical features. What is equally as significant, transmission along one cable does not interfere with transmission along another, even if the two are maintained at the same frequency.

The importance of this latter characteristic of cable transmission is that the physical constraint on the number of signals that can be delivered from and into a given area is at once removed. The frequency assigned to Channel 12, for example, can be used over and over again for any number of signals, so long as each signal is restrained within its cable, and reasonable separation is maintained between cables. Such a system is in principle infinitely copious.

But such a signal is not in fact a "broadcast" signal. If the signal emanates from a central transmitter, a coaxial cable must connect that transmitter with every receiver at which the signal is to be picked up. The system as a whole resembles a telephone system with its grid of telephone wires, except that the coaxial cable is the equivalent of several hundred telephone lines, and hence is substantially more expensive to manufacture and install. The enormous economy with which a single open-circuit transmitter can reach every receiver within an area of thousands of square miles is immediately lost.

Economies in cable operation begin to appear only when the density of receivers is great. A mile of cable will connect a single receiver to a transmitter that is a mile away. But that same cable can be tapped by receivers all along its path, and if there is a receiver every hundred feet, the same mile of cable (together with shorter lengths of cable to make the taps) will serve fifty receivers. Reconstructed to form a network of cable, with each tap from the trunk cable serving many receivers, the cost of the mile of trunk cable can be distributed among thousands of users. In areas of extremely high population density, such as the inner cores of large cities, the cost of cable connection becomes so small as to be relatively insignificant. This economy of scale has led in recent years to the construction of just such cable systems within large cities, where for a few dollars a month the set owner can shift from open-circuit to cable reception and thereby improve measurably the quality of his picture.

Current Uses of Cable TV

These cable systems are intimately linked with the present Television system. Under normal circumstances they carry exactly the programs which are carried by the open-circuit stations in the vicinity. For the most part, they provide no new services. But this is by no means absolute. A cable carrying twelve channels is little more expensive to build and maintain than a channel carrying three or four, and as a result the installation of a coaxial cable confers excess capacity on the system. That capacity can be used in various ways, one of which was mentioned above, and in some areas it is so used. But most of the capacity remains idle.

In existing situations, there is very little incentive to use the idle capacity. By definition, the channels which are merely retransmitting programs carried by the open-circuit stations are providing the most popular Television programs, for that is exactly the business that the stations are in. Whatever subaudiences may exist in the area are small, and whatever the dissatisfactions they may express, the harsh fact is

that they are tolerant of—if not delighted with—ordinary
television fare. . . .

New York could in fact enjoy the use of what may be
considered essentially an infinite number of channels, for
little cost, just as New York currently enjoys what is essentially an infinite number of telephones at little cost. It is
important to refer once more to the distinction between
television as a medium of communication and Television as
we are accustomed to regard it. In terms of customary Television, New York at the moment has in all likelihood the
maximum service it can afford, simply because there is no
further audience to support an additional station operated
on the scale of even the smallest independent. It is not further stations that New York can readily afford, but further
channels of communication. The difference between the two
must be kept firmly in mind. The question whether New
York wants, needs, or can afford more television stations is
not an issue. What might be asked is whether New York
needs more channels of communication. And what can be
said without hesitation is that if New York needs them, technology can provide them at once and at little cost.

It might be well to point out that the major part of the
system is already in being. There is no practical limit to the
number of channels that can be received on a conventional
television receiver. Every receiver now in existence can be
adjusted, at small cost, to receive twenty or forty or sixty or
more channels than the three or seven or ten that it now is
capable of receiving. That capital investment in the television set has already been made, and is constantly being renewed. And it will remain, under any circumstances, the
largest of all the investments in television.

The Instance of Bedford-Stuyvesant

It is within the limits of present-day technology to provide for such an area of New York City a far more copious
communications structure, and at the same time it is at least
questionable whether New York City, as a whole, stands in

need of such a structure. But the doubts vanish if attention is fixed, not upon the city as a whole, but upon certain areas within the city.

Bedford-Stuyvesant is a section of Brooklyn covering 653 blocks and housing nearly 400,000 citizens grouped into 100,000 households. The population is predominantly Negro, of the lowest urban socioeconomic strata. Of the total, a relatively small percentage are second-generation urban dwellers or more; the rest are either migrants from rural areas or the children of migrants.

Bedford-Stuyvesant is embedded in a larger community within which the various mass media are almost entirely at the service of the white middle-class population. This is particularly true of Television, which by the very nature of its operations is obliged to ignore any minority group, and in particular a minority group which is deficient in purchasing power.

In principle, the printing press provides unbounded channels of communication for Bedford-Stuyvesant; in practice it is only of minor significance. The reason is not far to seek. The use of print as a device for communication is a habit which must be cultivated within a society, and it has never been cultivated within the societies from which the New York Negro migrated, nor is it measurably cultivated in the societies to which they have come. Illiteracy is high among urban Negroes, but even the literate are likely to be "functionally illiterate" in large numbers: they can read, but do not.

The consequence is that there exists, within Bedford-Stuyvesant, no pervasive medium of communications by means of which the entire community can address itself to its common problems, its common needs, and its common aspirations, nor is there any pervasive medium of communication by means of which Bedford-Stuyvesant can organize to address the outside community or be addressed by it. Set down though it is within the country's largest city, and at the hub of the world's most elaborate communications complex, Bedford-Stuyvesant is nonetheless a community in isolation.

The consequences of such a situation are grave. It has disastrous effects, for example, on any attempt to erect responsible leadership within the area, for the responsible leader has no effective means of making contact with those whom he would lead. The way is left open for the street-corner demagogue, communicating by means of hysteria and violence, incipient or real.

The economic consequences are equally significant. It is difficult to disseminate information concerning employment opportunities, either within the area or outside it. The local entrepreneur lacks means of advertising his wares or his services. One lively area of employment, communications itself, is almost entirely unexploited.

Important means of creative and emotional release are absent. The Negro musician, the Negro artist, the Negro writer must seek any large audience through the agency of the white world outside his community; he is cut off from any direct tie with that audience. . . .

Dollars and Cents

For just such a community, cable television may provide an almost miraculous solution. For the functionally illiterate or the illiterate, it is the ideal medium of communications. The population density in Bedford-Stuyvesant makes it possible to envisage the installation of coaxial cable into every apartment at a price which is easily manageable. The receiving sets are already in place; some 90 per cent of all the households in the community already possess them. Specifically, a coaxial cable system capable of carrying twelve channels of wide-band signals could be installed in Bedford-Stuyvesant at a cost of a few millions of dollars. For this sum, cables could be laid that would connect each receiving set in Bedford-Stuyvesant to a central transmitting studio and that would provide also pick-up points within the community, other than the studio itself, from which signals could be transmitted over the system. . . .

None of this is in any sense visionary. The full technology is at hand for a twelve-channel system, and a larger system could be designed and built as quickly as funds were made available. The technology is fully mature. To erect in Bedford-Stuyvesant a multichannel communications system which would operate through existing receivers would be child's play for any reasonably competent engineering company.

It is exactly at this point, however, that the practical man raises his inevitable objection. "To build the system may be simplicity itself," he says. "But how on earth would you program to fill twelve channels, let alone twenty or forty? What could you possibly hope to transmit that would occupy that much capacity, or even a tiny fraction of it? Where would the great sums of money come from to produce the programs?"

The early sections of this essay have sought to make it clear that the question, sensible although it may at first appear, is in fact totally irrelevant. It is not proposed that the channels be "filled" by "television programs." It is not proposed that the channels be "filled" at all. It is merely proposed that they be available. . . .

Once more it must be stressed: this essay proposes the erection of channels of communication. It does not propose "Television for Bedford-Stuyvesant." Much of that is already provided by commercial open-circuit television; more could be provided, if that were held to be desirable, by buying or borrowing time on commercial or noncommercial television, or by establishing a station in and for Bedford-Stuyvesant. But that is not the issue here, for such provision would leave the communications needs of the area essentially unchanged. What is suggested here is the provision of means by which extensive mass communication can be carried on within the area and across its boundaries.

An Operating Structure

Assuming that a communications system such as that described might be created within an area such as Bedford-Stuyvesant, it is necessary to devise means of operating and maintaining it. Many operating structures might be designed: the one which will be set forth here is intended merely to suggest some of the problems that would arise and the mechanisms that might handle them.

It is proposed that a nonprofit corporation be created to manage and operate the system. Membership in the corporation would be drawn from the community. The corporation would own the coaxial cable and other associated equipment and would manage the terminal equipment by means of which the cable would be fed. It would be charged with maintaining the equipment. Its principal task, however, would be the provision of access to the system. . . .

As a general rule, the corporation would make its system available, at appropriate fees, to any potential user much as a printing press is made available. Provided that the applicant was of ordinary good standing in the community and that his projected use of the facilities was consistent with good taste, good judgment, the laws, and the general spirit of the community, use of the system would be made available at the customary schedule of fees. Since it is to be expected that the system would have at almost all times excess capacity, the problem of choosing between potential users would rarely arise; when it did arise, however, the corporation would make its decision on the basis of normal criteria: the order in which application was made, its own durable relationships with potential users, and the needs of the community as it sees them in its own best judgment.

The corporation would be prepared further to use its good offices in several ways. During the initial period of operation, it would stand prepared to aid potential users to organize their own efforts, and to bring them to fruition. Thus the corporation itself might seek out persons within the community prepared to organize and maintain some kind of employment service over the channels, and might assist in the early stages of such an enterprise by providing expert advice in both preparation and presentation of materials. The corporation would also stand ready to assist in the raising of money for preparation and presentation of materials, such funds to be sought from the government, from private foundations, and from individuals. It would be expected, however, that under normal circumstances the user of the facilities would be responsible over the long term for financing those activities.

It is also to be expected that materials would be simple and inexpensively prepared. The elaborate "programs" of commercial Television are rarely appropriate for the kinds of use suggested here; a camera and a speaker, or even upon occasion a camera trained upon a teletype, will often be all that is necessary. If it is protested that such materials are not "telegenic," it should be stressed once again that this is not a Television system but a communication system and that for the most part it is intended not to attract and hold an audience, but to serve its users. . . .

It is to be expected that government organizations would seek to make full use of the facilities. Among such organizations, one might expect the board of welfare and the various boards of education to make most effective use of the facilities, for which they would of course pay appropriate fees. Other users might include public health services, consumer services, and the police. There are also obvious opportunities for agencies serving the very young and very old. Initially, the corporation might find it necessary to stimulate such use by its own efforts; it is to be presumed that in time the most effective users would come to depend upon the system.

Because there is no constraint imposed by limited channels, there will be no need to judge users on the popularity of their efforts. Should the board of education, for example, be willing to pay its fee simply in order to reach a few thousand or even a few hundred illiterates, or those in need of special job training, there can be no possible objection to such use. The individual who might wish to rent a channel for thirty minutes so that he might make a speech would be quite free to do so, whether he was using the time and facilities to seek political office, to comment on the news, or to defend Bacon's authorship of Shakespeare's plays. He would, of course, in none of those cases have any assurance that anyone was tuned to him.

The set-owner would merely have access to new channels. The use made of that access would be entirely up to the set-owner. Those with the skill and the finances to make great efforts toward popular acceptance might, if their skills matched their intentions, win great audiences. That would be their privilege, and any rewards from their success would be theirs to enjoy. It might turn out that the channel utilized by the board of education went totally unwatched: that would be the concern of the board of education, and not of the corporation.

Why Not?

It is clear that the corporation would need, initially, a fair amount of venture capital. Over the first few years of the system it is highly unlikely that revenues would match costs; to aim initially for full recovery costs would only prevent development of the system. It would only be if and when the system proved both useful and workable that there might be an expectation that it would be on a self-sustaining basis. It should be considered possible, however, that in time it would become in fact a profitable system, deriving from its fees— even at minimum figures—far more than it expends. This would be a delightful outcome, and would raise only trivial problems that would become a pleasure to solve.

At the same time, it might well be that the system as a whole would prove unnecessary. In such a case, it would vanish quietly. The proposal here is truly that an experiment be undertaken; the proposal is made because it appears likely that the experiment would be useful. If it should be successful, a major contribution will have been made toward the solution of the problems of every major Negro ghetto in the country. It is not an expensive experiment, and it appears to be well worth pursuing.

WHAT ROLE FOR PUBLIC TELEVISION? [3]

There is a great to-do these days about "educational television"—visions of satellites, projections of a "cultural revolution" more revolutionary even than Mr. Mao's, a far-ranging congressional inquiry, a Ford [Foundation] Program, a Carnegie Report, a presidential proposal and, in general, a wide variety of dialogue, including a not-inconsiderable amount of static.

This large concern with the subject arises out of a belief that the state of the Union, informationally and culturally, is not what it should be and a conviction that television is not contributing what it could toward the advancement of that state.

Recent reports clearly indicate the information gap: three quarters of the American voters, it is reported, cannot properly identify the Vietcong; in a CBS current-events test it was revealed that, applying tenth-grade standards, nearly three quarters of those tested flunked the examination.

These are deeply disturbing findings. Democracy cannot truly function without an informed public opinion. The politician keeps his ear as close to the ground as the laws of physics allow; if public opinion is enlightened, national policy is likely to be sound; if it is unenlightened, national policy is likely to be both uncertain and unsound....

Because television has become a potent factor in American life, it can do vital jobs in the improvement of public opinion and the furtherance of public "culture" (the quotation marks are used not by way of apology but solely because

[3] From "A Program for Public-TV," by Lester Markel, a former associate editor of the New York *Times* and moderator of "News in Perspective," a semimonthly television program. New York *Times Magazine.* p 25+. Mr. 12, '67. © 1967 by The New York Times Company. Reprinted by permission.

the word has been tainted with pomposity; yet there is no other word). But commercial television has not done these jobs and is not likely to do them. Noncommercial television has done better, but its efforts have been limited by lack of funds and scantiness of audience.

The urgent assignment is to enlarge the size of television's minority audience—that segment of the watchers to which better programing appeals. This is not, in my view, an impossible task. Far from it; my belief is based on some sheer, wholly intuitive guesses: probably 20 per cent of the population are moronic; another 20 per cent are capable of learning, if they had the desire to learn, which they do not; another 20 per cent are really informed and culturally alert.

This leaves 40 per cent who are willing to learn if the learning is made simple enough and who are ready to absorb culture if it is provided in easy doses. The challenge lies in this gray area of the 40 per cent. The hope rests in the strengthening of Public-TV—of what President Johnson has called a "vital natural resource."

The Needs

What exactly is this TV apparatus we talk about? What has been its performance? Why has it not been better? What can be done? Most important, what can Public-TV contribute? These are the questions around which the debate focuses —a debate that now engages the educators, the Congress, the TV industry itself and, slowly, the public.

The reach of television is statistically breathtaking. The TV audience is reckoned at over eighty millions; Mr. Nielsen, one of the scientific samplers, estimates that 94 per cent of American households own at least one television set.

There are now in operation some 600 commercial stations, of which more than 500 are affiliated with the three networks [CBS, NBC, and ABC]. In 1965 the revenue of private television totaled almost $2 billion and profits before taxes almost half a billion. This is Big and Booming Business.

Noncommercial television comprises approximately 125 educational stations in the country; of these more than 80 are school or university or state stations which are devoted primarily to instruction (in this discussion, the instructional aspect of Public-TV is not considered; that is a separate operation and presents no real problem); some 40 are community stations, placed mostly in the large metropolitan areas, which present general programs. Most of these public stations are loosely affiliated with the National Educational Television network (NET), which supplies to them—with only occasional exceptions—taped programs.

At the moment, the contest between commercial and noncommercial television is a decidedly uneven one. On the one side, there is a Goliath armed with a shield of gold; on the other is a kind of David equipped with a puny stone, with no prospect that the outcome will be at all biblical.

Before any definite accounting of TV is attempted, these three primary aspects need to be ledgered.

First, for the large majority, TV is a medium of entertainment. Anything these viewers acquire by way of information or culture is incidental and almost accidental. Private-TV is intent on giving the public what it wants—or at least what it thinks the public wants. ...

Second, Private-TV, because it receives huge public grants from the nation in the form of licenses, should have a large dedication to the public service. But it has never paid more than lip service to the concept and the Federal Communications Commission has never made any sustained effort to force a shift in programing—for various reasons, the most important being the influence of the TV lobby in Congress. (Because of direct financial interest in TV stations or because of pressure from newspaper publishers who also own television stations or, most of all, because television appearances are vital for politicians, the TV industry gets favored treatment.)

Third, Private-TV has done some excellent shows and is fully capable of doing more, but, because of its commercial structure, it will not present enough of these programs and it will not assign enough prime time to those it does present. Therefore the task becomes one for Public-TV. . . .

Newspapers and TV Compared

A large responsibility for enlightening public opinion rests with the newspaper and television. They supply—or should supply—the information on which public opinion is based. When they fail, we have, instead of public opinion, apathy or, even worse, public emotion.

The newspaper is still the primary source of news. It has decided advantages over television: it can provide perspective; it has the authority of the printed word; it is constantly at hand, rather than requiring, as television does, presence at stated hours.

But newspapers, in too many instances, are not performing their true function, and an improvement in journalism is a prime need. But, even if that betterment is achieved, television has an important role to play. It cannot supplant the newspaper, but, because of its immediacy and its dramatic impact, it can supplement it to a significant degree. Yet television's news performance is far from satisfactory.

In on-the-spot coverage of events—the Kennedy tragedy, the adventures of the astronauts, outstanding sports contests —Private-TV does an often-superb job. But it does not provide interpretation of the news or perspective on it—and in these days of complex affairs, presentation of facts without an exposition of the meaning of those facts has little significance. Interpretation is essential and it must be done in graspable terms so that even the most hurried or elusive TV viewer will stop, look and listen.

The lack of background is especially marked in the evening news programs, which are almost wholly bulletin services. In what was heralded as a valiant effort, the Cronkite and Huntley-Brinkley programs were increased from a quarter hour to a half hour each evening. But the additional fifteen-minute segments have been given not to interpretation but to features which are often hardly relevant to the day's news.

The commercial stations provide a certain amount of local intelligence, but this is usually the same kind of triviality about persons and happenings that swamp the local newspaper—police-blotter stuff or "society news" (the quotes are an understatement) or the presentation of names in the hope of snaring readers.

As for news documentaries on Private-TV, which in the days of Murrow had wide impact, there are still occasional presentations that are aids to understanding, but they are few and they are decreasing. Moreover, such documentaries are likely to be belated and, being generally unmarketable, are presented at hours when most people are otherwise occupied.

Of the thirty-four new programs on Private-TV that were introduced for the season beginning . . . September [1966] not one was related even remotely to public affairs. The fact is that news operations are not rated as Bonanzas and so are relegated to the off-hours.

The Public-TV Record

Public-TV's performance in the public-affairs area is even worse; it has the hours but it lacks the content. There is little news and what there is, with few exceptions, is amateurish in concept and presentation and also failing in interpretation. Moreover, the absence of facilities for "live transmission" is likely to be fatal to almost any news broadcast.

Public-TV's documentaries—such as "A Time for Burning" [about urban ghetto riots] and the summaries of the Fulbright hearings [on China and Vietnam]—have been at times excellent and have shed needed light on long-term trends. But just as urgent are reports presenting without delay the background of events—and these are not being provided.

The gaping lack in television, then, is the effective presentation of news. If we are to be able to cope with the baffling problems of the world—possibly the several worlds—of the future, that lack must be remedied.

In the culture area, television, in view of the number of hours spent before the screen, obviously can have a large influence. The difficulty of the task should not be underestimated; yet it should not be overestimated either. The "cultural explosion" may be only in the lip-service stage, but it is at least a start, and eventually the bricks and mortar may be infused with spirit and out of shadow may come substance. Television, here too, has a large opportunity but, on the whole, it fails to meet the challenge.

As for Private-TV's performance in the cultural area, there have been periodic efforts to provide better fare, such as the presentation of *The Glass Menagerie* or *Death of a Salesman* or the "Hallmark Hall of Fame." But there has been an actual decline in the number of cultural specials, and of the . . . [1966-67] season's programs, only one had anything vaguely to do with culture. . . .

The performance of Public-TV in the cultural field has been more consistent; it has brought to listeners good plays, good music, good critical programs, such as *Uncle Vanya, An Enemy of the People,* and the series entitled "The Creative Person." But the money has not been available to carry out a really impressive schedule.

Moreover, too much of Public-TV's cultural programs have been designed for the small minority; and, too often, a local station, in the effort to be different, has presented indifferent offerings—so far off-Broadway that they are beyond reach or so close "in" that they stifle and suffocate.

Commercial television, precisely because it is commercial, will not really perform in the cultural area until public taste is considerably elevated, the public desire for better entertainment thereby stimulated, and thus the presentation of "culture" made profitable. But these situations are still far in the future, and so the task becomes one for Public-TV, which should be the Lincoln Center (or what Lincoln Center should be) of the television screen.

The Remedies

Now the faults are being recognized and remedies are being discussed. The debate has been stimulated by three proposals—that of the Ford Foundation, under the direction of Messrs. McGeorge Bundy and Fred Friendly, his T.V.I.P.; that of the Carnegie Commission, under the chairmanship of Dr. James Killian; and that of the President [Lyndon B. Johnson] in a special message to Congress.

The original Ford [Foundation] proposal was a spectacular; it suggested that a TV satellite be launched to serve both commercial and educational stations and pay for Public-TV out of the fees charged to Private-TV. But mathematics got in the way; it developed that the most revenue such an enterprise might produce would be some $30 million, whereas the cost of doing anything approximating a real job in Public-TV is estimated at more than $200 million. Subsequently, certain taxes were proposed to increase the total. . . .

The Carnegie Report also sees public television as a "great instrument" for the public good. It concedes—too easily, it is argued—that commercial television has not done and should not be expected to do this kind of job. It proposes two or more national production centers, but they are to be supplemental to the local stations, to which the primary responsibility for programs would be assigned. The whole enterprise would be carried on under the direction of a public corporation which would be entrusted with the task of raising the necessary funds, both from Congress and private sources—a proposal endorsed by . . . President [Johnson].

This is the essential difference between the Ford and the Carnegie philosophies: the Ford proposal puts the main emphasis on the national approach. It takes too little account of the function and needs of the community stations; the Carnegie proposal, on the other hand, exaggerates the po-

tentialities of the community stations; a central operation is
needed, because only it can supply the staff and the expert
touch required for effective programs in the public affairs
field.

The true approach is something between the two philosophies. . . . [President Johnson's] proposal seems to advo-
cate this course—a combination of the best features of each
of the two programs.

Thus the debate proceeds. But there is one extraordinary
and distressing fact about it: there is voluminous discussion
of the philosophy and mechanics of the operation but minimum consideration of the content. The basic question—what
can Public-TV contribute?—is almost submerged in the mo-
rass of rhetoric and technical lingo. What, then, can be done
in the way of content?

Because of the pressing need of a better informed opinion, the first assignment should be in the area of public affairs—in supplying news broadcasts, news documentaries
(extended news-background reports) and debates over current issues.

Most urgent is the presentation of the news in an understandable way. This means that there should be much more
than a bulletin service or background supplied long after the
event; it means daily broadcasts at prime hours, in which
the news would be given, and in perspective. . . .

Included in such broadcasts should be the presentation
of local aspects of national or international news (examples:
the way the Vietnam draft affects the community; or what
the Common Market means to the factory at Fourth and
Main Streets) or a discussion of community issues (examples: the problems of the local schools, of juvenile patterns,
of civil rights or analysis of civic virtues and vices
generally). . . .

The documentaries should adhere to the same general
principles; they should be done close to events so that the
impact of the headlines, and the consequent interest,
are not lost.

Thus a presidential message on the state of the Union should be followed almost immediately (as it was on NET) with a program that indicates where the proposals leave the Great Society program. Or an election in Germany with a program indicating what forces seem to be operating in the country and what this means for the future of Europe and for the world.

If the national network is staffed as a good newspaper is staffed—with experts in all the important areas—these tasks of interpretation can be carried out without delay, without waiting on the outside authority, who usually asks for time to arrange his affairs and to permit professorial cogitation. (It is my experience that in many instances delayed opinion holds no advantage in expertise over instant commentary; moreover, it lacks the dramatic appeal and the immediacy of the latter.)

A weekly, three-hour show, covering the high points of the news and dramatizing the significant happenings in every field, can be a demonstration of what Public-TV can do in certain areas. But it does not solve the day-by-day problems of the community stations, and it cannot possibly deal properly with the local issues that confront a hundred or more communities.

Finally, there are needed well-ordered and well-moderated debates over the pressing issues of the day. These must not be the usual symposia, with their free-for-all, unfocused discussions and with a half-dozen panelists striving to get a half-dozen words in edgewise. . . . I would opt for two protagonists able to provide maximum light with minimum heat.

Raising the Cultural Level

Greater efforts and new approaches are required also in the cultural area. One of the great problems of the future—possibly the greatest problem—is the use of nonworking time, which, as a result of automation, is likely to increase sharply. Work will be less stimulating; there will be a need for distraction or even the mere passing of time and for training and method in the use of leisure. Television will surely continue to play a large part in the program of living; it can provide leisure-time programs, and it can supply guideposts for other leisure-time activity.

What is needed is more theater, more music, more art, more discussion of books, more philosophy, if you will. This must be done both for the sophisticate and the uninitiated, in the hope that an increasing number of the latter can become interested. (For the theater, for example, a repertory company might well be a compelling idea. Repertory has not done well on Broadway for reasons difficult to fathom, but on television it might fare very well. There is a basic appeal about good actors playing a variety of roles; that has been amply proved in the movies and on the TV screen.)

None of this rules out entertainment; it suggests only that entertainment be supplied on a somewhat higher level. I believe profoundly that the public taste is far better than the pap-dispensers reckon it to be. If what is provided is not too far above its head, if the art and the music are not too recondite, if the drama is not too morbid or too remotely off-Broadway, I am sure the minority audience for culture will be largely increased. . . .

In sum, then, this is to be said: There is a large assignment for television. Some of that assignment can and should be carried through by Private-TV but most of the undertaking must be assumed by Public-TV.

Public-TV must break new ground and, in fact, achieve new approaches both in information and in culture. To be sure, it has suffered from lack of funds, but it should be recognized that finances alone will not do the trick; imagination also is required, for ideas are often more important than cash. That is why it is essential that the present debate be concerned much more with content than with mechanisms.

Above all, Public-TV must strive to increase the size of its audience. There is no point in preaching to the converted or ploughing the wastelands rather than the potentially fertile acres. Public-TV must attain, if not a majority, at least a large minority; and, in the course of the long road, set up markers to indicate to Private-TV what can be done that is at once inspiring and profitable.

Public-TV has the potentiality of being a "great instrument"; it should be wielded as such, as an essential part of the national service, in the effort to ensure that the nation will develop the kind of public opinion and cultural viewpoint which are the hallmarks of a true democracy.

THE SUBURBS DISCOVER RADIO—
AND VICE VERSA [4]

Three days a week in the early afternoons, housewives in Westchester County [New York] can hear a New Rochelle psychologist on radio station WVOX explain how to tell if their sons are homosexual or how to open the door on Halloween: "Smile a lot; that'll scare hell out of them."

Sunday afternoons, second-generation Hungarian-Americans in New Brunswick, New Jersey, tune in WCTC to hear the music of their ancestral homeland and commercials in Magyar and English for local eating spots (ethnic programs for Polish Americans and Italian Americans are also presented).

Long Island listeners with problems ranging from how to find out where the bluefish are biting best to what to do about the dog equivalent of diaper rash get answers to those questions daily on special programs on WGSM in Huntington and WGBB in Freeport.

Special, highly localized programing of this type is evidence of a renaissance in suburban or home-town radio in the New York area.

Listeners and advertisers are beginning to forsake, to some extent, the New York City stations—with their annual advertising revenue of $34 million—for the upper end of the

[4] From "Radio and Suburbs Discover Each Other," by Robert Windeler, reporter on cultural news. New York *Times.* p 24. D. 30, '68. © 1968 by The New York Times Company. Reprinted by permission.

AM dial (the more powerful lower and middle frequencies are dominated by metropolitan stations). Suburban stations, once the money losers of radio, are prospering as never before.

Reap Population Reward

To some extent, the ... commercial suburban stations are the beneficiaries of the continuing flight to the suburbs, but most have found a growth rate in recent months faster than their individual rates of population increase.

Advertising revenues have tripled on some stations in two years, and yearly increases of 30 per cent are now common. And responses to call-in shows and contests and other informal indications—few of the stations subscribe to surveys —show that listenership is up by 25 per cent or more in the last eighteen months—even in areas where the population is relatively stable.

Many stations ... are building or have recently built new plants or extensions, and most have added substantially to their station staffs, particularly in the area of local news coverage.

Virtually every AM station in a suburban New York, New Jersey or Connecticut town is, by its own calculation, No. 1 in its listening area by a wide margin, for as long as it is on the air—usually followed by New York City's No. 1, all-talk WOR—and the smaller stations that are AM only in the daylight hours find that they retain increasingly substantial portions of their audience when they switch to FM, with essentially the same programing, after sunset.

The general trend to suburban station prosperity began about two years ago, according to a consensus of station general managers interviewed in the greater New York area. ...

The change began when national advertisers, particularly gasoline companies, soft-drink suppliers and large department store chains, decided to place more of the advertising that had been on the New York "umbrella" stations (so called because they cover the whole suburban listening area) into the hands of the local stations. This took place in Los Angeles, Chicago and Detroit as well as in New York.

These national ads, which now account for as much as 35 per cent of a suburban station's revenue, were geared to local consumption—mentioning, for example, the gas stations in a given town along with the virtues of the particular brand. Many of the new suburban advertisers . . . had not even used metropolitan radio before, relying instead entirely on daily newspapers.

As national advertising has increased, so have station rates—in some cases as much as from $2.50 to $17 for a one-minute spot in morning "drive" time (6 to 10 A.M.)—but so have local advertisers, and station managers find that the only advertisers permanently squeezed out are family-owned grocery and specialty stores.

The attractiveness of local radio as an advertising medium coincided with the realization by suburban stations that they could never compete with New York stations in general music or talk show programing.

"We tried to be as hard rock as ABC," recalls William C. Mims, former general manager of WKQW (it was called WRRC in those days) in Spring Valley, Rockland County [New York]. "But everyone who wanted hard rock still listened to ABC and we had no one."

Most suburban programing had leaned heavily toward what William O'Shaughnessy, thirty-year-old president of WVOX in New Rochelle, calls "blue-skies-Westchester-suburban—background music" or to pale imitations of William B. Williams's low-key intimate music and chitchat show on WNEW. Then came community involvement in a big way.

"Operation Snowbird"

The stations, some under revamped or new management, began to program more of what they thought were, or what listeners told them were, local needs. Music—what the trade calls middle-of-the-road (usually from *Billboard* magazine's Easy Listening Top 40)—was still offered, and it was modern enough to appeal to young marrieds but not loud enough to make them tune out. But for Mr. O'Shaughnessy and others, "Music is strictly subordinate to hell-raising and involvement in our community."

Some of the community involvement is so specialized as to seem trivial to any town but the radio station's own (what ponds in Pompton Lakes have ice safe for skating, what parking lots at Jones Beach have empty spaces)—and therein lies the real secret of local radio's new success.

Weather is the single most important point of public information and "people on Long Island don't want to know about the weather in Central Park," Richard J. Scholem, general manager of Huntington's WGSM, notes.

"Snow made this station," Jean Ensign, a comely blonde who is executive vice president and general manager of WVIP in Mount Kisco says. "Operation Snowbird," a service announcing school, road and industry closings and the areas of deepest drifts and swiftest winds, started with the station in the winter of 1957-58 and is now so complex that planning for it starts in August (each school in the area has a responsible person with a secret code number authorized to call the station, to prevent pranksters from saying school is closed when it isn't).

WVIP, housed in a cluttered snailshell-shaped building in the woods of northern Westchester, is only on AM during daylight, but listeners can get the latest weather at any hour by calling a special number at the station for a recorded report on local conditions. From October 1, 1967, to September 30, 1968, 239,353 of them did just that—at the rate of one every two minutes, twenty-four hours a day, 365 days a year.

So that its fourteen-member full-time staff can concentrate on local news, WVIP has just signed the American Broadcasting Company's Information Network for national and world news, making it one of the few New York suburban stations to have any network affiliation.

Mrs. Ensign finds it preferable to spend the extra effort on local features like "Memo Pad," twenty minutes a day of free announcements from more than five hundred organizations, and "Pet Parade," which helps find northern Westchester's lost cats and dogs and once located a pet peacock (it was sitting in a tree) and three lost pigs with rings in their ears.

When Mr. Mims took over WRRC in January the station was losing money at a rate he'd rather not talk about. It had an image of nothing but juvenile music in the midst of the affluent well-educated medium market (potential audience: 250,000 to 300,000) that is Rockland and three surrounding counties.

Believing that "it's a conglomeration of small-to-medium market radio stations that forms public opinion in this country," Mr. Mims changed everything including the call letters.

"Not changing them would be like taking a shower and then putting on the same underwear—we'd still be smelling," he says. WRRC became WKQW.

Network of Correspondents

WKQW now has editorials on all subjects and a network of high school students and suburban matrons who serve as part-time reporters (some without pay, some for as little as $5.00 an assignment, but all with station press cards) and five full-time local newsmen.

With this emphasis the twelve-man daylight-only station has tripled its advertising revenue in eleven months. Mr. Mims left it this month to look for another station to rebuild. . . .

Henry S. Hovland, general manager of WGCH in Greenwich [Connecticut], thinks the success of his and other suburban stations is not service or even snobbery, but "seeking an identity in megalopolis, not for the stations, for the people; they resent being swallowed up."

Perhaps the most aggressive, certainly the most flamboyant of suburban stations is Mr. O'Shaughnessy's WVOX in New Rochelle. Just three years ago the AM-FM outlet was "twelve desperate people in a bomb-shelter basement," the

general manager says, and a $5,000 to $6,000 a month tax
loss for Whitney Communications.

Today WVOX is still in the basement—albeit refurbished
—but prospering as southern Westchester's soapbox, taking
sides in every dispute and having "great faith in Mrs. Jones."

Last month the station started a two-hour Saturday afternoon program devoted to black listeners (the only such program in New York suburban radio) conducted by Luther
Vinson, an assistant to the president of the Freedom National
Bank in Harlem and a self-described "responsible militant."
Mr. Vinson has total control and costs are being borne by
the station until a sponsor is found.

GROWING INFLUENCE OF BLACK RADIO [5]

"Say it loud, baby. I'm black and sure enough proud
of it."

Speaking into the microphone, paraphrasing the title of
a James Brown hit, is Chris Turner, a Memphis [Tennessee]
disk jockey.

He sits in a small cluttered studio of radio station WDIA
(Theme: "More Soul Power per Hour."), whose programing
is aimed at the black community. He wears a Dashiki (an
African style shirt) and when he's not playing records on
Memphis's most popular radio station, he devotes most of
his spare time to a militant group ("we don't do any burning
up or anything like that") called the Black Knights.

The twenty-two-year-old disk jockey and his colleagues
around the country work for a rapidly rising number of lu-
crative, mostly white-owned "soul stations" beamed at the
black community. The audience is estimated at 25 million,
of which about 5 per cent is white.

Approximately $35 million worth of advertising is placed
with these stations annually. In 1960 the figure was
$10 million.

[5] From "Black Radio Stations Send Soul and Service to Millions," by
Robert E. Dallos, reporter on cultural news. New York *Times*. p 64. N. 11, '68.
© 1968 by The New York Times Company. Reprinted by permission.

Today [1968] there are 528 stations programing anywhere
from an hour to the entire broadcasting day for blacks, an
increase from 508 last year and 414 in 1964.

Of these, 108 stations aim all of their programing at Negroes, compared with 50 eight years ago and only one in
1947, according to Howard Bernard Company, a New York
company that sells advertising for thirty-five black-oriented
stations. All but eight of the black stations are owned by
white interests.

The soul stations play mostly rhythm and blues music—
a few play only gospel music—and the disk jockeys are almost
exclusively Negro. Musical performers, both live and on
record, are also generally black and most of the commercials
are made by blacks in a familiar idiom.

Jive Talk Disparaged

Coca-Cola, for example, makes a number of rhythm-and-
blues commercials for black radio using recording stars, including Aretha Franklin, Joe Tex and Ray Charles. Kent
Cigarettes uses the black Chicago disk jockey Ed Cook (Nas-
sau Daddy) to narrate some of its commercials and rhythm-
and-blues groups to provide the music, and Lou Rawls does
the commercial for Cold Power detergent.

"Our men have to speak well," says Zenas Sears, the
bearded, white vice president of WAOK, one of Atlanta's
three black stations. "It's been clean up the language or get
off the air in this city. No more *y'all* or other jive talk. Racial
pride is a very important part of the business."

Soul stations are also devoting an increasing number of
hours to discussions of topics of special interest to blacks.
The programs enable community leaders—both black and
white—to talk to the stations' large audiences and they allow
frustrated blacks to call in and "sound off."

In New York, WWRL, for example, broadcasts a weekly
ninety-minute talk show entitled "Tell It Like It Is," during
which listeners may call to take part in discussions on such

topics as "Welfare in New York City," "The Negro and the Draft," and "The Ghetto School Crisis."

Another WWRL program focuses on Negroes who have successful careers. It is titled "Spotlight on Your Future" and sponsored by Lever Brothers Corporation. It is designed to "show youngsters in disadvantaged areas what they can achieve with proper education and training."

New York's other black station, WLIB, won a Peabody Award, one of broadcasting's highest honors, for its "Hot Line" program.

Soul stations have also been performing other important community functions. These vary from city to city and depend on local needs.

KXLW in St. Louis, for example, gives thirteen weeks of spot announcements to Negroes starting businesses and WCHB in Detroit helped find food, clothing and shelter for victims of the 1967 summer riot.

But there are critics who say that the efforts of many white-owned Negro stations take the forms of "safe" public service. For example, one critic who asked not to be identified, said the stations run campaigns urging black children to stay in school, but they would do little to lead and organize movements to correct the underlying conditions that cause the youngsters to fall behind and quit.

Helping to "Cool It"

After the assassination of the Rev. Dr. Martin Luther King, Jr., . . . [in April 1968], most black radio stations dropped all their advertising and played only religious music and reports concerning the murder. They were cited by officials in many areas of the country for having helped to avoid local disorder. . . .

Station KGFJ in Los Angeles was praised in a city council resolution for having been "instrumental in keeping racial trouble from developing" and maintaining "a helpful, informative approach to assist in easing tensions when any trouble did have an opportunity to blossom."

But it is the music, news and chatter of the black stations that have proved extremely popular and caused audiences to increase rapidly.

Washington has a 63 per cent black population, and most of its members are regular listeners of station WOL. In addition, WOL also has a fairly large white audience, mostly teen-agers. As a result the station has maintained its number one position in the twenty-three-station area for the last two years.

The same is true in other cities. In Memphis, WDIA has been the top rated station of twelve for years as is WVON in Chicago.

The spending power of the nation's 22 million Negroes is currently running at $35 billion annually, according to the Department of Commerce. By 1970 the figure is expected to reach $45 billion.

And major companies are now recognizing this. There are almost two dozen concerns, according to the Howard Bernard Company, who spend $100,000 a year advertising on Negro radio. These include General Foods, Colgate-Palmolive, Humble Oil, General Motors and R. J. Reynolds.

The Sonderling Broadcasting Corporation, which owns four black stations, recently raised its advertising rates from $10 to $52 a minute in Washington (WOL), from $20 to $36 in Memphis (WDIA) and from $18 to $60 in New York City (WWRL).

"Over-all Negro radio is a cheap buy," says William Lilios, the Howard Bernard Company's director of research. "In cities like New York, Chicago and Washington general market stations with comparable-sized audiences charge two to three times as much."

The revenues of Atlanta's WAOK will near $600,000 this year, according to Mr. Sears, compared with $450,000 in 1966. Sonderling's Oakland, California, station, KDIA, was grossing $165,000 a year when the company acquired it in 1959. Currently it is grossing between $600,000 and $700,000.

But while many advertisers are flocking to black radio, some local advertisers—notably restaurants, banks, clothing and department stores—are boycotting black radio for fear of attracting too many Negroes and consequently losing their white customers.

One of Atlanta's five largest banks has refused to advertise on WAOK, according to Mr. Sears. He declined to identify it for publication. "They just don't want the Negro business," he said. "They tell us: 'A few we don't mind. But we don't want too many.' " He adds that some clothing stores still boycott the station and a large car dealer canceled an advertising campaign recently because too many Negroes turned up at its show rooms.

But a spokesman for the bank in Atlanta about which Mr. Sears complained, said that his institution had advertised on black radio when a specific appeal was being made to the Negro community.

The inherent problem [he said] and we hope it will be solved soon, is that the average income level of the Negro is still too low. There are certain things blacks are not in a position to buy. They don't have checking accounts, they don't have that much money.

WDIA's manager, Bert Ferguson, who founded his station twenty years ago and stayed on after selling out to Sonderling, says his ad salesmen are often told "we're glad to have those [blacks] who come into the store. But we don't want to make a specific appeal. It would have a bad effect on the market we're used to."

Robert Elliot, director of radio for Atlanta-based Rollins, Inc., which operates four black stations, says two or three businesses in Norfolk, Virginia, still refuse to advertise on its station, WRAP. But he notes that a bank—he declined to identify—that had always refused, signed on last month for the first time because "it realized the significance of the black business."

There's been a gradual loosening of restrictions by local advertisers [Mr. Ferguson said]. The reason: The civil rights movement and the plain and simple fact that the Negro has more money to spend.

Public Service Function

Perhaps one of the most important functions of black stations is the public service they render. This was recognized by Nicholas Johnson, a member of the Federal Communications Commission, who recently told a convention of black disk jockeys that it is not enough to play soul music.

Soul radio is big business [he said]. It is also big responsibility. Many institutions have tried to reach the destitute and alienated millions who seek a richer future in the hearts of our cities. The schools have tried. The Office of Economic Opportunity has tried. Newspapers have tried. . . . Only one institution has consistently succeeded. That is Negro-oriented radio.

Memphis station WDIA, founded in 1947 as the first radio station to devote itself exclusively to blacks, has long broadcast along personal lines.

For example, the following public-service announcements were made recently on the station's "Night Hawk" show.

A billfold was lost at the bus station, 1324 Kennedy, contained money and papers. Call 9461708.

A small brown German shepherd dog strayed from home. Dog answers to the name of Poochie. Mrs. Edna Grayson of 1451 Parkway South is offering a $10 reward for Poochie.

WDIA's Bert Ferguson says that

this might all sound silly to whites. But whites have their daily newspapers and whites have more money. To a Negro the loss of a $3 umbrella is a major loss. We will run anything that has to do with the Negro community in Memphis.

Other black stations perform similar public service work.

One important way that many blacks are aided by the stations they listen to is in finding jobs.

Radio station KATZ in St. Louis broadcasts local job opportunities five times a day. And WVOL in Nashville, which has been broadcasting job openings for some years, is currently campaigning to get what it terms "upgraded job offers for Negroes." In Augusta, Georgia, WAUG broadcasts job offers directly from the state employment office.

News and editorials concerning items of interest to the black community are also carried by most soul stations, WAOK, for example, carried taped interviews with Julian Bond, the Georgia legislator, from the Democratic National Convention, and with other black delegates.

Some stations, though, are wary about putting news items on the air when they concern racial disturbances.

> Our news is screened [says Robert Meeker, the white president of KCOH in Houston] so that when an individual with treasonous motives says "go out in the street and kill and burn," we do not report this.

WERD in Atlanta bans all news of racial unrest while such incidents are in progress.

> The news policy of this station [said Bert Weiland, the white vice president and general manager] is not to report violence of any kind while it is going on. I strongly feel that TV and radio contribute to the incitement of riot. I do not consider this censorship.

But WERD believes it is serving the public interest with another type of broadcasting. Six times a week it produces two-minute vignettes about the contributions of blacks to American history under the title of "Our Noble Heritage." These are made available to black stations in other parts of the country.

AMERICA'S NEWSPAPERS—A CRITIQUE [6]

The death [in 1967] of the short-lived *World Journal Tribune,* New York's fourth journalistic casualty in four years, has renewed the perennial search for the killers of the American press. I have my own pet culprit, one I consider more lethal than abysmal labor-management relations, the

[6] From "What's Wrong with American Newspapers?" by A. H. Raskin, assistant editor of the editorial page of the New York *Times.* New York *Times Magazine.* p 28-9+. Je. 11, '67. © 1967 by The New York Times Company. Reprinted by permission.

movement of the well-to-do from center city to suburb, the upsurge of television and news magazines or any of the other more proximate causes of death in the recent fatalities in New York.

The real long-range menace to America's daily newspapers, in my judgment, lies in the unshatterable smugness of their publishers and editors, myself included. Of all the institutions in our inordinately complacent society, none is so addicted as the press to self-righteousness, self-satisfaction and self-congratulation.

That, needless to emphasize, is a personal view, not widely shared by my colleagues. At the risk of outdoing Uriah Heep in my smug antismugness, I feel there is a need in every paper for a Department of Internal Criticism to put all its standards under reexamination and to serve as a public protector in its day-to-day operations.

The press prides itself—as it should—on the vigor with which it excoriates malefactors in government, unions and business, but its own inadequacies escape both its censure and its notice. The credibility gap is not a White House exclusive; it also separates press and people. There is disturbing skepticism among large groups of readers, including many of the best educated and most intellectually alive, about whether what they read in their newspapers is either true or relevant.

It is easy enough to shrug off the laments of public officials chronically convinced that they are insufficiently appreciated by their journalistic assessors. Certainly no correspondent or editor will feel obliged to lock up his typewriter when President Johnson grumbles that "there is something about our open society that gives the play to what went wrong instead of what went right." Or even when Vice President Humphrey weeps over the image of America the world gets from press preoccupation with air bombing in North Vietnam and race riots at home.

But it is harder to dismiss the observation of Ted Soren-sen after returning to private life:

> In the White House I felt sorry for those who had to make judgments on the basis of daily newspapers. There's a large dif-ference between reading diplomatic cables and intelligence reports and sitting in your living room reading the papers. Now I'm one of those guys sitting in his living room reading the papers and I'm even more acutely aware of the difference.

An acerb footnote comes from another refugee from the White House, Arthur M. Schlesinger, Jr. He told the Ameri-can Historical Association that, after being in on the making of history, he could never take the testimony of press reports on such matters seriously again. "Their relation to reality is often less than the shadows in Plato's cave," he declared. Of-ficial miscalculations in Vietnam, the Bay of Pigs and other peril points demonstrate that government intelligence re-ports can themselves be the foggiest of guides, but their un-reliability does not vitiate the Sorensen-Schlesinger comment. It merely underscores the essentiality of an alert and inde-pendent press to explain what the world is all about.

Journalism Without Scholarship?

No week passes without someone prominent in politics, industry, labor or civic affairs complaining to me, always in virtually identical terms: "Whenever I read a story about something in which I really know what's going on, I'm as-tonished at how little of what's important gets into the papers —and how often even that little is wrong." The most up-setting thing about these complaints is the frequency with which they come from scientists, economists and other acade-micians temporarily involved in government policy but with-out any proprietary concern about who runs the White House or City Hall.

Their contention is not that the press is getting worse but that it is not getting better fast enough to keep up with the radically altered nature of news. "We live in the midst of a continuous and multidimensional revolution, and today's new ideas are tomorrow's hard realities," was the way McGeorge Bundy, president of the Ford Foundation, put it in a recent talk to the American Society of Newspaper Editors. He suggested that many professors could tell more of the important daily truth than the conventional star reporter, and added:

The professions of scholarship and of journalism are threatened with a requirement of merger. A cynic might say that the scholars should learn to write and the journalists should learn to think.

One reason the press doesn't worry more about how well it does its job is that the profit statements of most daily papers make pleasant reading for their owners. The *World Journal Tribune* drowned in red ink; indeed, it had been born out of the monumental deficits that engulfed its forebears—the *Herald-Tribune,* the *Journal-American* and the *World-Telegram and Sun.* But their lugubrious financial experience was the final spasm of a shakeout that has all but extinguished press competition in New York and most other cities and has left the great bulk of the survivors, large and small, in exuberant fiscal health.

The number of dailies has remained at roughly 1,750 through all of the two decades since World War II, with the shrinkage in the metropolitan centers balanced by the rise of flourishing new papers in the suburbs. Combined circulation climbed 20 per cent to a record high last year of 61.4 million. That growth, made while television was moving from laboratory experiment to household universality, is in line with the increase in adult population between the ages of twenty-one and sixty-four. What takes much of the comfort out of the statistic, however, is its indication that newspapers merely held their own despite an education explosion that sent book sales skyrocketing and should have provided a comparable spur to public demand for information about local and world affairs.

The sensational growth within the newspaper field has been in advertising, which brings the average publisher three to four times as much revenue as he gets from circulation—even with higher newspaper prices. Since 1949 press advertising income has risen from $2 billion to a current national total of $5 billion. Television, almost a stranger to Madison Avenue in 1949, now sells commercials to the tune of $2.75 billion a year. But even when magazine, radio and billboard advertising is added to the TV figure, newspapers take in almost half of all the dollars people want to spend on making other people want to spend more. The big explanation lies in retail advertising, mostly from department stores, which accounts for more than 50 per cent of the newspaper figure. When help wanted, houses for sale and other classified ads with a distinctively local appeal are added in, the ratio rises to 80 per cent—all in areas where up to now television, radio and magazines have shown little capacity to produce dividends for advertisers.

Troubles of the Press

Even with the fatter ad take, however, many papers have been unable to keep up with the escalating cost of news coverage, newsprint, labor and everything else that goes into production and distribution. The advertisers themselves have been selective; they have concentrated on the papers with the class or mass, shutting out those they considered laggards as sales activators. Archaic union rules have blocked automation and discouraged investment in modern plants; long strikes have convinced many readers they could live without newspapers. Obtuse, indifferent or absent owners have caused papers to lose touch with their communities or to cling to news patterns that went out with hand-set type. And, once a paper edges into the red, the tendency is to push it further toward extinction by economizing on the only thing that gives it any reason for being, its news coverage.

The result has been a growing trend toward the survival of a single newspaper or a single publisher operating both morning and afternoon in most American cities. In 1947 this movement toward press monopoly was noted with concern by a Commission on Freedom of the Press financed through a $200,000 grant by Henry Luce and headed by Dr. Robert Hutchins, then chancellor of the University of Chicago. It warned that the power of the press giants was growing, and added: "They can advance the progress of civilization or they can thwart it. They can play up or down the news and its significance, foster and feed emotions, create complacent fictions and blind spots, misuse the great words and uphold empty slogans."

When that dirge was written, there were still 117 cities with competing daily papers. Today there are only 65 out of a total of nearly 1,500 cities, and even in 21 of those the force of competition is diluted by the operation of joint printing plants, circulation, advertising and business offices. New York, Washington and Boston are the only cities left with three separate publishers, and many observers believe Boston or Washington may come down to two in the next few years. Of the country's 50 largest cities, 23 have single newspaper ownership.

It is no longer fashionable, however, to suggest that there might be something unhealthy about this trend toward concentration. The current line is that the squeeze-out of marginal papers not only is inevitable because of the high costs of operation but also is a godsend to the public because it enables papers to do a much more comprehensive and responsible job for their readers and their communities.

Unquestionably, there is substance to the contention that the absence of competition has impelled some publishers to invest more in covering local, national and foreign news and has freed them from any compulsion to sensationalize in the interest of stealing readers from a rival. In Milwaukee, Minneapolis, Louisville, Atlanta and Des Moines papers have got better, not worse, under monopoly ownership.

But the fact that only five or six dailies in competitive cities compare with those sheltered blooms in journalistic excellence does not make the swoop toward exclusivity any less dangerous in terms of democratic values. The most conspicuous lack in all our big cities is in understanding urban problems and in originality and diversity of ideas on how to solve them. To say that a single journalistic voice offers the best insurance of adequacy in that direction is nonsense, and it is even more fatuous to argue that the availability of TV, radio and news magazines eliminates the need for more than one newspaper. Indeed, the only time publishers are disposed to acknowledge that the electronic media can approach newspapers as vehicles for education in community affairs or for comprehensive information about the world is when they want to impale the dragon of press monopoly on a convenient TV antenna. Where the monopoly publisher also enjoys a TV and radio monopoly, there is, of course, no shadow or shield for diversity.

Death of the World Journal Tribune

All the things that bother me about the trend to mergers and monopoly were gruesomely illustrated in the *World Journal Tribune*. It was the bloodless synthesis of a dozen papers that, over the period of almost a century and a half, had reflected the boldness, imagination and even genius of such towering individualists as Joseph Pulitzer, William Randolph Hearst, Horace Greeley, James Gordon Bennett, Charles A. Dana, E. W. Scripps and Roy Howard.

No spark of their spirit seems ever to have entered into the negotiations that led to formation of the WJT, a paper born to die. The representatives of Hearst, Scripps-Howard and Whitney Communications, as interrers of their three lacerated New York standard-bearers, were so conscious of the money already sunk in them that considerations of profit and loss dominated the premerger talks.

The original plan was to make a stab at keeping two of the three papers alive, although no one was very san-

guine that the morning entry, the *Herald Tribune,* could
stay alive long against the *Times* and the *Daily News.* The
ten newspaper unions took care of any doubt about how
long by calling a strike for greater job security that aborted
the morning paper before it got out its first issue as part of
the pooled corporation. The 140-day tie-up left the afternoon paper a cripple so weak that orphaned members of
its own staff called the management decision to put it out
of its misery after eight months a "mercy killing."

The unions, of course, had their standard alibi: "We
didn't kill it; it committed suicide." When the first spasm
in the interminable tests of strength between the New York
unions and the publishers began with a 114-day citywide
strike in 1962-63, seven metropolitan dailies were involved.
Now the number is down to three, and no one yet seems to
have learned anything from the carnage. "Both sides deserve
each other," was former Mayor Robert F. Wagner's classic
description of the relationship after he had devoted most
of 114 days and nights to helping settle the initial go-round.

Lunatic as were its labor aspects, the most depressing
aspect of the WJT debacle to me was the lack of any dis-
cernible misgivings on the part of the three partners, each
supposedly possessed of a strong sense of journalistic mission,
about their ability to sleep contentedly in a single bed. I
suppose that is the answer: It was their intention to sleep,
not to visualize their homogenized product as a living thing
with heart, soul and voice to rouse the community. How
else could the same editorial page embrace the "Stars and
Stripes Forever" traditions of the Hearst chain, the somewhat faded liberalism of Scripps-Howard and the moderate
Republicanism of Whitney?

The mixture that came out of the malted-milk machine
was just what you would expect. Bland, characterless. All
three bosses kept hands off; no editorial board ever had
more freedom or did less with it. Frank Conniff, the Hearst
alumnus who was made editor-in-chief, got turned down
only once. He felt one way to make an impact was to have

the merged paper come out for [New York City] Council President Frank O'Connor in his race to unseat Governor Rockefeller ... [in 1966]. It turned out all three publishers were for Rockefeller, so that decided that. The paper was a mishmash of columns, features and news, with no integrating flavor or personality.

Conniff sought to exorcise the Hearst image by playing down stories about "Go-Go Girl Slain" or "Rapist Hunted." That cost him a lot of the lowbrow trade and the paper never could develop enough sparkle or authority to build up much of a highbrow or even middlebrow following. Nonetheless, it went down with almost 700,000 Monday-to-Friday readers, the fourth largest evening circulation in the nation, and it would have had up to 50,000 more if its ancient mechanical facilities and the hazards of Manhattan traffic had not cut the ceiling on how many Wall Street closing editions it could get to Grand Central and Penn Station before all the commuters were gone.

Rich Papers—Without Character

One obvious moral from the WJT experience is that newspapers must stand for something if they are to succeed in a period where the price of being second-best is extinction. Unfortunately, like all tidy morals, this one doesn't stand up too well. It is true that you can point to some excellent papers which are moving from one peak of prosperity to still higher ones by concentrating on ever higher standards of editorial quality and community usefulness. The New York *Times* and the Los Angeles *Times*, on opposite sides of the continent, are symptomatic of perhaps a dozen papers in this category. The Washington *Post, Wall Street Journal* and St. Louis *Post-Dispatch* also shine as papers and as profit-coiners.

But in monopoly cities it is possible to point to scores of papers without distinction which are making money so fast you would think they are running greenbacks rather than newsprint through their presses. Vincent J. Manno and his associate, George Romano, two of the country's most active newspaper brokers, report an extremely strong market for large and small newspapers, with buyers far more plentiful than sellers.

The most spectacular success story of the past half-century is that of Samuel I. Newhouse, who has built an empire of twenty-two newspapers with an estimated worth of more than $300 million out of a 1922 investment of $49,000 in a half-interest in the Staten Island *Advance*. The astonishing part of the story is that Newhouse doesn't even pretend to have a personal philosophy of journalism. His principal contribution to his papers is in overhauling their business and production practices; he stays out of their editorial and news policies on the theory that these can best be handled by local management. Some of his papers are Democratic, others Republican. He has 18 million readers, many of them in cities without competition, but the business side of the operation is all that engages his personal interest.

"The agencies of mass communication are big business, and their owners are big businessmen," the Hutchins Commission declared in its strictures on press monopoly twenty years ago. But it costs a lot more to start a daily now than it did then. In fact, it costs so much and the odds are so heavy against any independent seeking to break into an established newspaper market that the usual advice Manno and Romano give their clients is, "Don't start, buy."

Newhouse paid $42 million five years ago for a New Orleans monopoly, the *Times-Picayune* in the morning and the *States-Item* in the evening. This year he bought Cleveland's only morning paper, the *Plain Dealer*, with only 375,000 circulation, for $54 million. Anyone who attempts to start a new afternoon paper in New York will need an initial nest egg of $25 to $50 million, and even then he will probably have to enter into a mutual production arrangement with the *Times* or the *News* to hold down costs. Even in relatively small cities or suburbs, papers command sales prices of $10 or $15 million.

All of which makes it plain that the press, exercising a right to publish guaranteed by the First Amendment, cannot sit on an ivory throne and insist on immunity from community comment or criticism in the same manner that it might if it were still possible for every itinerant owner of a hand press to set up shop and compete in the area of news and opinion.

Resentment, Disdain, Indifference

When the Hutchins Commission found newspapers failing in their obligation to give the public "a truthful, comprehensive and intelligent account of the day's events in a context which gives them meaning," the reaction of most publishers was apathy or anger. Professor Zechariah Chafee, Jr., of Harvard Law School, a commission member, recorded in *Nieman Reports* the only suggestion for improved news coverage put forward at the annual meeting of the Associated Press after the commission's 1947 reproach. He said the chairman's request for ideas on how the AP could do a better job had brought a long silence, broken at last by one man's proposal that the agency start carrying news of the Irish Sweepstakes.

A combination of resentment, disdain and indifference remains the characteristic response of most newspaper nabobs to suggestions that the health of their balance sheet is not an infallible gauge of the adequacy of their performance. Thus, when Ben H. Bagdikian, after several years of research into the strengths, foibles and frailties of American newspapers, wrote in the March [1967] *Esquire* that "trying to be a first-rate reporter on the average American newspaper is like trying to play Bach's *St. Matthew Passion* on a ukelele," his most emphatic rebuke came from the curator of a foundation set up to promote higher journalistic standards. Dwight E. Sargent of the Nieman Foundation accused Bagdikian of hashing up glib assumptions, gross exaggerations and myths.

But a much more pungent indictment of American papers came a few weeks later from the publisher of the most popular morning paper in the world, Britain's *Daily Mirror*, a breezy tabloid with more than 5 million circulation. Cecil King archly informed the American Society of Newspaper Editors that this country was producing "unreadable, unmanageable newspapers without a message or with one which is effectively muffled." He called them "the shabbiest product in a land which has shown the world how the best designed and most elegantly finished goods can be produced cheaply for the masses."

King reserved his sharpest barbs for the extent to which news had become a thin layer of filler to keep ads from bumping together. "After the first page or two in the typical American paper," he said, "all you get is a rivulet of news flowing sluggishly by a wide meadow which has been leased to some department store or supermarket." And just to rub it in, the incongruity of it all: "Young women prance in underwear against a column recording famine in India or an analysis of the Kennedy Round." . . .

For all the overkill in the King description, the problem of keeping ads and news in some reasonable balance gets more troublesome for all papers as costs push through the roof and advertising pays a bigger share of the total bill. In 1946 the average daily had 27 pages, of which 12.3 went for editorial content and 14.7 for ads. Last year the size of the average paper had almost doubled to 53 pages, but ads got 18 of the new pages and editorial content only 8. Where the two had started almost even in total space, there was now a ratio of better than 3 to 2 in favor of ads.

It is, of course, easier to tune out an ad in a newspaper than it is a commercial on TV; all you have to do is turn to the next page—and the next ad. It is also true that ads are the news for a lot of readers, especially women; what the stores are selling is what they most want to know. But many papers are approaching the point where the reader has to have a derrick to help lift them on Sunday and where he needs one bus seat for himself and another for his paper on weekdays. The saturation level may be at hand on newspaper size; the crucial question then will be whether the ratio can be maintained or reversed in favor of news.

Much more fundamental, however, is what improvements newspapers can make in their own assessment of news and how it fits into the snarled web of modern existence. The equanimity with which many people took the recent strikes in New York, Detroit, Toledo and other major cities has made it plain that newspaper reading is a habit people can get out of. If newspaper quality disappoints or if electronically transmitted information gets better, even monopoly may not create a privileged sanctuary for newspapers.

Right now the press scoffs at that possibility.

We no longer fear TV but welcome it [declares James L. Knight, board chairman of the Knight Newspapers]. We have learned that the story only half-told or half-heard on TV likely will have the greatest readership in our newspaper the next day.

But Fred Friendly, moving into public television, says it a bit differently:

Broadcast journalism is going to destroy newspapers—bad newspapers—all of them. Just as TV benched all the bad sports broadcasters of radio days, TV is going to retire all the bad newspapers.

A New Approach to News

The old definition of news as "anything you learn today that you didn't know before" has been receding for quite a while under a recognition that newspapers have to be something more than vacuum cleaners spewing a great blob of undigested facts on the reader's breakfast table every morning. Now the accent is on understanding and on meaning, on putting the facts into the framework of the reader's interest and experience.

Desirable as that endeavor is, it is plain that the transition from the old focus on hard news to the current concern with perspective and background is creating a good many distortions in its own right. Part of the problem is that too many reporters forget that a full knowledge of the facts is essential to sound interpretation; they are sent into a strange field or country and within twenty-four hours are writing highly subjective analyses of what everything means, including a good many things that never happened. Others stay longer—and do the same thing.

A related imbalance stems from wedding the new techniques of depth reporting to the perpetual obsession of newspapers with the "news" value of the aberrational. In its attempt to turn the spotlight on every significant new trend in the society and thus give its readers an insight into the real world, the press often comes up with images as twisted as those in a funhouse mirror.

By way of example, listen to Dr. Seymour L. Halleck, director of student psychiatry at the University of Wisconsin, explain why a growing number of students are beset by a sense of boredom, meaninglessness and chronic unhappiness.

There is a tendency for mass communication media and the arts to focus upon the most extreme behaviors in our society and present them as though they were the norm. Alienation is a favorite subject. The student learns quickly that adopting the alienated role provides him with a certain amount of status and attention.

This kind of criticism is not an argument *against* perspective reporting; it is an argument *for* perspective reporting. Interpretation is not an assignment for those too lazy to dig out the facts officials seek to hide or too dull-witted to understand the facts when they get them. The good analytic reporter in science, urban affairs, civil rights, education, politics or international relations is the one who weaves a pattern of comprehensible reality out of the crazy quilt of dynamic development that is incessant in all these fields.

Joseph Alsop, who has been making his own highly personalized appraisal of the world through his Washington column since 1935, believes the big trouble with the press is exactly the same as Congress's trouble with the executive branch. It hasn't kept up with the problems and so it can't "peg even" with the Administration's experts in trying to find out the things the White House doesn't want it to learn.

Despite all the security rules and other obstructions, the man who has bothered to master his subject can still go out and get the information [Alsop says]. Carter Glass once said to me of William Jennings Bryan, "That goddam nincompoop thinks that any man with real goodness of heart can write a banking act." And that's the whole mistaken theory of journalism. They think that any man with real goodness of heart can write a banking act. A huge professional corps of experts has grown up in the Government. You can get a great deal of information out of them, but you must be able to peg even—not just go in and ask a Sinologist, "Tell me all about China."

Part of the task of getting with it lies outside the realm of redefining the scope and nature of news. It involves making sure that the press is not left without either medium or message by its antediluvian technology. Many newspapers, especially those fettered by the craft-conscious recidivism of unions whose skills would be obsolete if they did not exercise a veto over the future, are still in what columnist Jimmy Breslin calls the skate-key stage of composing-room practice. In non-union centers like Los Angeles, Oklahoma City and Miami, computers are setting type and performing other operations without any wholesale annihilation of printers' jobs. But even those forward steps are timid approaches to the all-electronic newspaper of 1975 or 1980.

At the last meeting of the American Newspaper Publishers Association . . . [in 1967] Professor William Kehl of the Massachusetts Institute of Technology envisaged a reporter sitting at a remote console about ten years from now typing a dispatch direct into a computer in his home office; an editor would read and edit the copy from the same computer, which would then set the story for publication and perhaps even transmit a hard copy into a subscriber's home by way of his television set or some specialized receiver.

A variety of such direct-to-reader techniques, bypassing all the traditional printing crafts, are on their way to feasibility. Some would enable you to pick the particular news items you want from an index shown on your video screen and then dial them in for reading in your easy chair or at your desk. Others would entail home delivery of all or selected parts of a facsimile newspaper through a pseudo-printing plant inside your TV.

The unanswered question is who will get there first with practical devices of this type—the TV industry or the newspaper publishers—or will somebody outside the present monopoly structure of mass communications score an end run on both? Whoever it is, don't expect him to be a suppliant of the Small Business Administration. Perhaps in preparation for this technological scramble or perhaps because their cash position makes it a good idea, several of the most solvent publishers are strengthening their over-all holdings by branching out into book publication, the preparation and distribution of educational materials and even the acquisition of more newspapers in suburbs and major cities. This tendency of dominant publishers to seek to extend their dominance has brought some signs of apprehensiveness from the Justice Department, and one antitrust test is currently under way against the Los Angeles *Times* in connection with its absorption of suburban papers in southern California.

Needed: Flavor and Conviction

Whether newspapers are competitive or unchallenged, they cannot amount to much in their communities unless they have flavor and conviction. Most editorial pages are so predictable in position and so pedestrian in style that they seem to have become the first part of the paper to be completely automated. They speak without passion or persuasiveness, as if in self-abnegating default to the army of columnists who have now moved into the role of opinion-influencers. In this proliferation of columns the aim of many publishers seems to be to neutralize all their syndicated pundits by covering the full spectrum from right to left with cave-of-the-winds completeness. The conscientious plower through this maze of mentors is more likely to emerge with vertigo than enlightenment.

There are more imaginative ways than the pyramiding of columnists for publishers to make certain that their papers are hospitable to a range of comment, criticism and ideas broader than their own. Almost half the country's papers are owned by chains, groups or other absentee owners; that makes it doubly important for them to accord at least as much attention to providing a forum for exchanging views and clarifying goals of all groups within the community as they do to parading national columnists to cancel out one another.

That is the point of my proposal that newspapers establish their own Departments of Internal Criticism to check on the fairness and adequacy of their coverage and comment. The department head ought to be given enough independence in the paper to serve as an ombudsman for the readers, armed with authority to get something done about valid complaints and to propose methods for more effective performance of all the paper's services to the community, particularly the patrol it keeps on the frontiers of thought and action. Maintaining a "letters to the editor" column scarcely constitutes full recognition of a city's right of access to the paper that boasts of itself as the community's window on the world. And certainly not when one of the individual citizen's most persistent anxieties these days is how to keep from losing both his way and his identity in the mammoth institutions of a society of bigness.

In the debate over collision between the constitutional rights of a free press and fair trial, the legal profession has shown much greater openmindedness than the press on how best to protect both freedoms, much less tendency to take refuge in self-serving sloganeering. The medical profession, under the pressures of Medicare and Medicaid, has moved a long way out of its self-anointed role as a secret society aloof from any public accountability. Newspapers can even less expect to stand aloof.

There are signs—but not enough—that they are beginning to put aside the curious double standards that always have made them proclaim "the public's right to know" everything about everything except what goes on in the inner councils of the publishers themselves. The industry's most important conference, the annual meeting of the American Newspaper Publishers Association, used to be forbidden ground to working reporters. In recent years the great bulk of the sessions have been thrown open to the press. However, those devoted to exchange of views on the state of the newspapers—a subject of some interest to their 61.4 million readers—remain off limits except through second-hand briefing conferences. Peter Kihss of the *Times* news staff files a formal request each year for the right to sit in on these sessions. Each time he is turned down—on the ground that he would merely be bored by what he heard.

Newspapers are still too full of nonstories, hallowed by tradition but conveying no illumination to those persistent enough to read beyond the headline. Typical are the thousands of interviews, starting on the day after every Presidential election, in which all the future candidates dutifully get it on record that they are positively not interested in running for the presidency the next time around.

The most hopeful sign on the journalistic horizon is the extent to which some of the best established papers are resisting the temptation to believe that they can plod along well-paved paths in this era of ferment when nothing is precisely what it seems and truth wears a different face for each recorder. These papers are lifting the standards of quality at every level; they are attracting bright new talent, even though the best of newspaper salaries remain low by contrast with those in advertising, television, the sciences or industry generally.

But the problem of how to tell the news meaningfully—how to provide perspective without blotting out the line between fact and opinion—remains an ill-solved one. And unless it is solved, newspapers will lose both their best people and their readers. There never has been a time when good newspapers have been more needed; there never has been a time when it has been so hard to make them as good as they must be.

THE UNDERGROUND PRESS: A NEW WRINKLE [7]

There is nothing very underground about the underground press. The newspapers are hawked on street corners, sent to subscribers without incident through the U.S. mails, carefully culled and adored by the mass media. About three dozen of them belong to the Underground Press Syndicate which is something like the AP on a small scale; through this network they spread the word about what is new in disruptive protest, drugs, sex. Their obsessive interest in things that the "straights" are embarrassed or offended by is perhaps what makes them underground. They are a place to find what is unfit to print in the New York *Times*.

The Berkeley *Barb*, the *East Village Other*, the *Fifth Estate*, the *LA Free Press* are among the more familiar and successful of the papers. They make the aging *Village Voice* —of which they are all derivative—seem very Establishment indeed. The hippie thing brought them to flower; but the death of hippie (the funeral was in early fall and the obit was in *Newsweek*) has apparently not diminished them. They are all the things their admirers think they are—exciting, informative, In, irreverent, refreshing, audacious, lively; they haven't sold out like everybody else. But they are also recklessly undisciplined, often badly written, yellow, and, taken in large doses, very very boring.

The Most Exciting Reading in America?

Nevertheless these papers have been said to provide the most exciting reading in America. At least they try—by saying

[7] From "The Seedier Media," by David Sanford, associate editor. *New Republic*. 157:7-8. D. 2, '67. Reprinted by permission of *The New Republic*, © 1967, Harrison-Blaine of New Jersey.

what can't be said or isn't being said by the staid daily press, by staying on the cutting edge of "In" for an audience with the shortest of attention spans. There is nothing worse for an underground paper or its readers than to be the last to know. It took months for the revelations about the psychedelic pleasures of smoking banana peels, for instance, to travel to the daily papers and news magazines. And by the time a few weeks ago that the daily press reported that scientists had concluded it was all a hoax on the hippies, nobody who reads the *East Village Other* particularly cared. They had gone on to other things. They could sneer and remember they had been at the source, at the beginning of that long trip through the media to obsolescence.

The underground press is a photographic negative of the bourgeois newspapers and magazines; it registers many of the same images but all the colors are reversed. Anyone who sat down a few years ago and asked himself what isn't being reported, what causes are without champions, what words can't be printed, then decided to put out a newspaper that did everything differently, would have invented the underground. What the *LA Times* is for, the *LA Free Press* is likely to be against. Daily papers report arrests, for example, but from the standpoint of the police. That is their mental set; they are in the law-and-order bag. The underground papers are prone to see arrested persons as *victims* of the cops:

On Friday between 8 A.M. and 8:30 A.M. Judy (an antiwar protester) was arrested at the intersection of 13th and Broadway. She was standing with a group of people in the intersection. A cop knocked her down and grabbed her. A group of protesters circled the cop and began arguing that she hadn't done anything. More cops arrived. The cop who had knocked Judy down then let go of her. She began to move down Broadway and was chased by the cop who knocked her down again and dragged her to a patrol car. She was charged with assault on an officer.

Here the Berkeley *Barb* in simple, letter-to-a-friend didactic style leaves no doubt about its position on the police. Cops

attack innocent girls and charge *them* with assault. No phony
balanced coverage. No on-the-one-hand-on-the-other-hand
TV documentary stuff. Judy is *Barb's* friend. The negative is
black and white—a corrective to all the news about unruly
demonstrators and police officers trying to maintain order.
Police brutality has become a shibboleth for the underground papers, serviceable and pat. The treatment people
get at the hands of police is "rough," "completely unnecessary," "totally unprovoked." Cops are dumber and less imaginative than we usually suppose."

Disestablishmentarian

Since alienation is their thing it is understandable that
underground papers sometimes seem to reject bourgeois
journalistic values of accuracy and balance. The . . . [1967]
Pentagon demonstration as reported by the Washington *Free
Press*, for example, included bayonetings, demonstrators
who were knocked unconscious, the Pentagon as an "isolated
house of death" rather like a gas oven in Nazi Germany.
Such flights into fancy are characteristic of this spontaneous
freak-out journalism, the purest lode of which is to be found
in the *Oracles*, colorful Los Angeles and San Francisco publications, which are all mind excursion.

The underground press often reads like some kind of
Harvard *Lampoon* parody of the tabloid press complete with
news stories, editorials, reviews, classified ads, and advice
columns. But instead of Heloise there is Hip-pocrates (Dr.
Eugene Schoenfeld) —the motor-cycling, demonstrating MD,
whose syndicated advice appears in several UPS papers. . . .

The underground press is predictable. Some papers are
more political, others more psychedelic, others more aber-
rant, but for the most part they care about Dow, drugs, the
draft, abortion, cops, rock, flicks, and sex, perhaps not in that
order. They are as current as this week's pot bust and draft-
card burning. They oppose the war and their most interesting features are their want ads, especially if you are a sadist
looking for a masochist.

III. SOME ACHIEVEMENTS AND SHORT-COMINGS: THE MASS MEDIA AND THEIR CRITICS

EDITOR'S INTRODUCTION

No doubt it is the "mass" in "mass communications" that sparks the most bitter criticism. When the media play to that lowest common denominator described as "the average American," critics across the land can be seen climbing the nearest wall. Can culture survive—let alone thrive—in such a climate?

That question raises in its train a host of others. Is profitability a proper guide to performance for the mass media? Does the fault lie with the public—and "what it wants"— or with the so-called media barons? If the public prefers entertainment to news and public affairs, does it also prefer entertainment *in* its news and public affairs? Is TV news, for example, too dependent on the "star system"—the Huntleys, Brinkleys, and Cronkites of the airwaves?

This section examines some of the salient controversies surrounding the mass media today. In the first article a professor of journalism at Syracuse University describes what's right and what's wrong in the mass media today, and poses some questions that must be answered if the media are to meet the challenge of tomorrow. Next, a member of the Federal Communications Commission, Nicholas Johnson, questions the trend toward corporate concentration in communications, wondering whether a democracy such as ours can be safe when information is increasingly concentrated in the hands of a few "media barons."

In the the third article an advertising copywriter with broad understanding of television as a business explores six myths commonly associated with television criticism.

If you think that wicked advertisers, stupid sponsors, or deceptive audience ratings are responsible for bad programing, he claims, you are wrong. Next, a former TV journalist in New York, Robert MacNeil, offers an insider's critique of television newcasting. An answer to some of his charges, by Reuven Frank, executive vice president of NBC News, ends the section.

WHAT'S RIGHT—AND WRONG—IN THE MASS MEDIA [1]

Taken as a whole and with all their faults, the mass media in the United States, many authorities agree, are the best mankind has seen. Through newspapers, magazines, and broadcasting, more people are given more information than in any other country in history. Through them, each man's recognition that he is involved in all other men's lives, which is one of history's great change-making ideas, has been vastly expanded. As never before and nowhere else, the mass media have done the job given them by James Madison: " A people who mean to be their own governors, must arm themselves with the power knowledge gives." Government regulation of the media is at a minimum—perhaps too much. Financially, they are in robust health. Through them, diverse and unpopular opinions are expressed and spread, less than idealists wish and more than bigots can abide. They have both contributed to and fostered cultural expression and may even have improved the public taste—*may* have.

Most of the numbers that index the health of the mass media are up and climbing. Although big-city mourners regularly lament the death of newspapers, just about as many daily papers are being born in the suburbs as are dying in the cities. The total number has remained nearly constant for twenty years while the number of readers of daily papers

[1] From "The Mass Media—A Need for Greatness," by André Fontaine, former writer and editor, now associate professor of journalism at the Newhouse Communications Center, Syracuse University. *Annals of the American Academy of Political and Social Science.* 371:72-84. My. '67. Reprinted by permission.

has increased faster than the population. Advertising revenue has nearly quadrupled in the same time and now totals nearly $4.5 billion—more than magazines, radio, and television combined. . . . One index of the financial health of newspapers is that it is becoming almost impossible to find a daily paper for sale at a feasible price today.

Magazines, having passed the crisis in the 1950's that took the lives of many, are back in bursting good health [although the venerable *Saturday Evening Post* folded early in 1969—Ed.]. Circulation of magazines was "increasing faster than the growth of the U.S. adult population," according to the Magazine Publishers Association, while advertising revenue for the [year] 1966 was 7 per cent over the previous year.

Broadcasting was equally prosperous. According to the 1967 *Broadcasting Yearbook,* total time sales of both radio and television for 1966 were $2.5 billion, up nearly $200 million from 1965. . . .

This is fine, because when the mass media are run by private enterprise it is generally true (with exceptions) that the financially healthiest newspapers, magazines, and broadcasters do the best and most responsible jobs. They can afford to; an editor who has a little leeway in his budget is not under quite so much pressure to print only the surefire, and usually less responsible, material—if he is truly an editor and not a money man.

Less Bias, More Responsibility

With all their faults, the media are more responsible today than they were half a century ago. There is less bias in presentation of news, less venality, broader coverage of national and world affairs, more—but not enough—presentation of complex events in a perspective that makes them meaningful to readers and viewers. Even television, which has been the least conscious of its responsibility as an information medium, is showing some signs of recognizing its obligations. Professor William A. Wood, of Columbia University's Graduate School of Journalism, recently estimated that about 30 per cent of television and 20 per cent of radio stations "have reached the point where they do more than give routine attention to news and show real responsibility and quality in news services." ["The Sound of Maturity." *Columbia Journalism Review*. 4 no 4:7. Winter '66.] And in the list of things they are doing he includes the use of more special-beat reporters by local stations, more regular hours of news programing, more community service during emergencies, more local editorials by broadcasters, and more investigative reporting by stations in half the cities in the country's top fifty markets. . . .

All this is good; it is not great, and it is not even good enough. The rosy generalities mask a number of failures which, though varying in the different media, apply in some measure to all three. These failures must be repaired if the media are to achieve greatness.

Credibility Gap

When journalists produce material that their readers reject, they are no longer in the communications business.

Readers do not believe because what they are told contradicts their own experience. Recently the labor editor of *Business Week* opined that, with less than a half dozen exceptions, there are no labor reporters working for the mass media. Reason: the media ignore labor except when there are strikes, and then their reportage is often antilabor.

This makes no kind of sense. Some 13.5 million Americans are members of unions; most remain members because the union benefits them. They live through the wrestling over individual grievances, the campaigns for bargaining, and elections of union officers; at union meetings they argue out the endorsement of political candidates and their positions on local issues; they are told about—and often support with money—the struggles of other union members locked in a showdown with management, and some of them know the desperate frustration of being trapped in a racket union where venal leaders and employers conspire to exploit them.

Yet they read virtually nothing about this whole aspect of their lives in the mass media. Or else what they read, their experience tells them, is distorted. . . .

Recently, the publisher of a successful Negro newspaper in Baltimore said on a National Educational Television program that the reason he had been able to start and operate his paper profitably was that Baltimore's big newspapers had ignored Negro news. They were far from the only ones in the country which did, even though Negroes make up 10 per cent of United States population.

People are not stupid; obviously they conclude that the media cannot be trusted. If this distortion goes on too long, or occurs in a controversy that is too bitter, their distrust may spread to everything that the newspaper or magazine prints, and they reject it wholly.

But more often they are selective in their disbelief. They may believe what a newspaper prints on its women's pages, or a magazine in its service section, but be quite untouched by either's political reportage.

A More Critical Audience

People disbelieve because they are better educated today . . . [and] because, under the ceaseless drumfire of advertising and public relations, they are much more sophisticated than media practitioners think. This sophistication enables them to spot a phony message as far as the eye can see, and they detest being fooled. Thus, to the ancient abjuration that journalists must be unbiased for ethical reasons is added the warning that bias simply does not work. You lose your audience.

Recently the Syracuse, New York, papers ran a shrill, one-sided campaign opposing free state medical aid for the indigent. Many of the stories were written by a reporter named Luther Bliven. After some weeks his paper received—and printed—a one-line letter which said "Please keep Mr. Bliven's editorials off the front page." An informal survey of some three hundred residents of all socioeconomic levels in the same city at about the same time revealed that the majority thought that the papers were biased and therefore unreliable. One woman said: "I'm a Republican and they're on my side. But still they ought not to be biased."

Lou Schneider, who writes the "Trade Winds" column for the Bell-McClure Syndicate, criticized editors in the October 15, 1966, issue of *Editor & Publisher* for printing too much good news about business. He wrote:

Editors own stock and also they do not want to upset local department store management and other advertisers. If the story is not bullish, they simply get another story—140 business editors use the PR Wire [news service] publicity stories. No one writes the shady side of the street. . . . Yet readers want knowledgeable news they can depend on. There are 21 million investors in New York Stock Exchange stocks alone and they want straight news about what is happening and what is likely to happen.

When they do not get it, obviously they conclude that the media are not leveling with them.

There is no complete answer to this kind of audience skepticism, simply because no one knows precisely what kind of information people disbelieve or why. The best partial— and too general—answer is found in the old principle of fairness and impartiality. If the people believe a paper or magazine is leveling with them, they accept a good deal of difference of viewpoint without rejecting the entire publication.

The second half of the answer is that editors and writers must know the realities of their readers' concerns, and not let publisher's policy prevent coverage of it.

There is, for example, a general feeling among readers that advertisers determine a medium's policy. Yet scores of editors and writers have said things like: "Never in my thirty-five years of work has an advertiser influenced anything we have printed." Both are right. The advertiser's influence is subtle and pervasive. Any journalist smart enough to find the right keys on a typewriter quickly learns the taboos, and learns to work within them so surely that he forgets about them. But the readers do not.

If there is an answer, it is probably a lesson that was first learned a quarter century ago by the New York *Daily News*. A large advertiser objected to something the paper had published and threatened to withdraw its ads. The editor told him to go ahead. The ads were withdrawn, the paper felt the loss, but continued to publish. Within three months, the advertiser asked to come back into the paper and was accepted. The lesson which too many media executives, particularly broadcasters, have not learned is that advertisers need a truly independent publication more than it needs them.

Handling the Information Explosion

Information, of course, is simply another word for knowledge, and the increase in the sheer bulk of knowledge is one of the revolutionary changes of our time. It has often been said that the total of human knowledge gained since 1940 equals the amount gained in all the years of human history up to 1940. Some specialized areas have far outstripped others; physicists know, for example, that the quantity of new knowledge in their discipline is doubling every decade. And the social sciences generally are among the leaders in the totals of new learning.

As these areas have grown, they have, of course, become more and more specialized, and researchers in them have come to use language that is more and more esoteric and less and less comprehensible to the layman. A major part of the journalist's job is to serve as a communications bridge between the specialists and the average reader. In recent years he has done more of this in all media than ever before, but measured against the skyrocketing totals of knowledge his performance has been a roman candle against a Saturn rocket.

It is trite to point out that television is greatly overbalanced in providing entertainment as against information. . . .

Despite a few outstanding exceptions like improved half-hour news programs on the networks and truly distinguished reporters like Walter Cronkite, Edward P. Morgan, and Eric

Sevareid, the quality of information programs is superficial and episodic. The magazine *Broadcasting* reported (July 25, 1966) that the Columbia Broadcasting System (CBS) offered to provide three and a half minutes of world and national news to go into late-night local programs to 192 of its affiliates; only 31 were interested, and the offer was dropped. The *Columbia Journalism Review* (Spring 1966) likewise pointed out that when local stations were given a chance to reject news material on the Vietnam war they did so "in substantial numbers."

Even Columbia Professor Wood's upbeat report on improvements in radio and television news, cited earlier, found increased responsibility in only 20 and 30 per cent of stations —something less than a majority. . . .

Today's informed, sophisticated reader demands informed, sophisticated writing and editing. The magazines learned this twenty-five years ago, and the best newspapers are now following their lead—but only a few and only the best. The name of the technique is interpretive, or depth, writing. In it a trained and skilled writer examines a complex situation—juvenile crime, slum housing, water pollution, a seemingly senseless murder—studies the background in the library, talks to experts, interviews people involved, and comes up with what, in his judgment, is the essential truth of the situation. Then he writes his story in a way that gets the reader emotionally involved even as he learns the facts. In writing it, he borrows many of the techniques of fiction writing, and even showmanship, but is bound always, of course, by fact.

This is a difficult, highly skilled, creative kind of writing. It takes time and space, and it costs money, but magazines have built multimillion circulations—and millions for their owners—on it, and the newspapers found in anybody's list of the nation's best ten have done likewise. The *Wall Street*

Journal was an early innovator, and its offshoot, the
National Observer, does it consistently today. . . .

Shaking Off Old Ideas

Most newspaper editors complain that they have not the
time, the staff, nor the money for this kind of writing. They
do not have the time because they are still shackled by the
old idea that a newspaper must be first with the news—in an
age when it is impossible for them to beat radio and television with the story. They do not have the staff partly because they do not train their writers to do the job—or have
them trained. And they do not have the money because editorial departments on newspapers are traditionally short-
changed in their budgets. Yet it is the editorial department
that produces the most important service a newspaper has to
offer, and the one which makes the press the only private
industry whose freedom is guaranteed by the Constitution.
Without it the paper becomes a shopper's guide—which is a
perfectly legitimate publication, but is not a newspaper.

Allen H. Neuharth, general manager of the Gannett
Newspapers, told a group of editors on June 21, 1966, that
"you can increase your editorial costs by 50 per cent and still
not increase the over-all production cost of the paper." How
low editorial costs are in relation to others is shown by an
examination of 1965 figures from Inland Daily Press
Association.

On papers of 120,000 circulation and over, editorial costs
were half (11 per cent) of the cost of the paper they were
printed on (23 per cent of the total cost). This disparity
gradually decreased as circulations got smaller; at 22,000-
27,000 circulation they were about equal and at circulations
under 4,000—a very small daily—the editorial department cost
twice as much as the newsprint. The lesson is obvious—more
money needs to be spent on editorial departments. . . .

If all editors in all media were given the power they need,
most would see to it that they got the kind of writing skill the

media must have and would give the writers both training and time enough to do the journalistic job that is needed today.

Most would also see to it that young writers are recruited and trained. The media, driven by an annual need of five thousand new journalists, are just beginning to recruit in the universities; more advanced industries have been doing it for decades. And the media are just beginning to see to it their best writers get advanced training to equip them for specialized reporting and writing. At that, most of such training is financed by foundations, universities, or the writers themselves. In contrast, most progressive industries have been sending their promising young men back to college at their expense for at least a decade. . . .

There is little sound knowledge of where people get their information. What there is suggests that the media provide a small percentage of that information. A study by Stanford University of where people first heard of the assassination of President John F. Kennedy, found that nearly half (49 per cent) learned it not from radio or television, not from a newspaper, but from another person.

There is little or no research on precisely how sophisticated the media's audience is and on what kind of information it wants. Present categories in which editors present information—national, crime, sex, sports, and the like—may be outdated. Are they? If so, what new categories should replace them as rules of thumb for editors to apportion the contents of their publications and programs?

There is virtually no reliable information on the effects that the media have on the cities they live in. Does a first-class newspaper or broadcaster give its city a better government? more industry and jobs? a healthier cultural climate? better informed and more active citizens? If so, how? . . .

The Really Difficult Questions

If these and other gaps in knowledge are filled, if editors use it and are given the power they need, if writers get the

time and training they need, then the media may at last
begin to face some of the really difficult questions:

*To what extent has newsmen's reportage only of the dramatic
distorted their readers' concepts of reality?*

It is an ancient rule of journalism that when nothing hap-
pens there is no news. If this was ever true, it is no longer. For
decades, Negroes lived in slums with rats and garbage and
fear, their men jobless, their children uneducated; it went
unreported in the mass media until their desperation drove
them to violence.

For decades, police, lawyers, and judges have known that
there are two kinds of justice in America, one for the rich and
one for the poor; was that not news?

In many communities, for decades, real estate brokers,
builders, and contractors have had such control of local government that zoning, building, and sanitation codes were
either nonexistent or ignored; the situation and its effects
were known and unreported by the media.

For decades, our water and air have been quietly and
inexorably polluted; where were the reporters?

The answer that the local Establishment which controlled
the press was not interested in these matters is too easy; for
there are always journalistic Davids who aspire to giant-
killing. But these stories take time and perception and digging and thoughtfulness to get, and, with rare exceptions, the
media have not made the requisites available.

Can any editor say with certainty that if these and similar
situations had been reported, the people's view of their world
would not now be different? or that Watts might never have
revolted?

*To what extent has the media's endless exploitation of vio-
lence made violence so prevalent in America?*

Last August [1966] after Charles Whitman killed fifteen
persons in Austin, Texas, Charles Collingwood reported from

London that the British were sickened and saddened by their cousins' seemingly incurable addiction to violence. No modern Western nation in the same time span has killed as many of its heads of state while in office as America, according to Professor Carl N. Degler, Vassar historian. Every two minutes some American is killed, beaten, or wounded, said Senator Edward Kennedy recently. Has the endless recitation of crime and death on the front pages, the ceaseless depiction on television of the Old West, where violence is shown as a legitimate means to an end, had nothing to do with this?

To what extent have the media contributed to the increase in promiscuity and the cheapening of sex?

Thoughtful observers have pointed out that the rush to end the strictures of puritanism and the constant sexual titillation of the media have led people, particularly the young, to engage in sexual relations as fun and games. But sex without the care and concern and responsibility of love is as shallow and unrewarding an escape as alcoholism or narcotics. In encouraging it, how well have the media served the true human values of our society?

To what extent have the media contributed to the popularity of extremism and to the devil theory of international relations?

Any thoughtful review of the McCarthy madness [i.e., the late Senator Joseph McCarthy of Wisconsin] must conclude that if the media did not create McCarthy, they certainly increased his influence. Sober editors wonder, in hindsight, what would have happened to the Senator if they and their colleagues had simply refused to print stories about him. But, in the realities of competition, could they have?

Probably not. But while they reported his demagoguery they could have seen to it their readers also received enough perspective to be able to recognize it for what it was.

McCarthy was a loud and extreme exponent of the devil theory in international affairs—the simplistic idea that everything we do is right, but everything our enemy (currently communism) does is evil. But he was not the only one, either while he was alive or now. Professor Henry Steel Commager, of Amherst, described this well:

What we have here is a deeply ingrained vanity and arrogance . . . fed by isolation, by school histories, by a filiopietistic society which is that we are somehow superior to all other nations, morally and practically, by a thousand editorials, a hundred thousand radio and TV programs which play up the villainy of our enemies—the Russians, the Chinese, the Cubans—and our own morality and nobility.

What editor can say in conscience that he has not contributed to this illusion?

Bernard Kilgore, of the *Wall Street Journal,* has said:

The newspaper editor of tomorrow will be an egghead . . . the newspaper of the future must become an instrument of educational leadership, an institution of intellectual development—a center of learning.

Speaking May 10, 1966, at the fiftieth anniversary of the Pulitzer Prize awards, James Reston of the New York *Times* said:

Somewhere there is a line where the old skeptical, combative, publish-and-be-damned tradition of the past . . . may converge with the new intelligence and the new duties and responsibilities of this rising and restless generation. I wish I knew how to find it, for it could help both the newspapers and the nation in their present plight, and it would help us believe again, which, in this age of tricks and techniques, may be our greatest need.

This, then, is the challenge: it is the media's job to illuminate the values of American life, both the false and the true, and to use all their skill and technology to instruct and guide and lead the people into a less anxious and more rewarding way of living. Progressively, as they do this they will answer the need for greatness.

THE MEDIA BARONS AND
THE PUBLIC INTEREST [2]

Before I came to the Federal Communications Commission my concerns about the ownership of broadcasting and publishing in America were about like those of any other generally educated person.

Most television programing from the three networks struck me as bland at best. I had taken courses dealing with propaganda and "thought control," bemoaned (while being entertained by) *Time* magazine's "slanted" reporting, understood that Hearst had something to do with the Spanish-American War, and was impressed with President Eisenhower's concern about "the military-industrial complex." The changing ownership of the old-line book publishers and the disappearance of some of our major newspapers made me vaguely uneasy. I was philosophically wedded to the fundamental importance of "the marketplace of ideas" in a free society, and a year as law clerk to my idol, Supreme Court Justice Hugo L. Black, had done nothing to weaken that commitment.

But I didn't take much time to be reflective about the current significance of such matters. It all seemed beyond my ability to influence in any meaningful way. Then, in July 1966, I became a member of the FCC. Here my interest in the marketplace of ideas could no longer remain a casual article of personal faith. The commitment was an implicit part of the oath I took on assuming the office of commissioner, and, I quickly learned, an everyday responsibility.

Threats to the free exchange of information and opinion in this country can come from various sources, many of them outside the power of the FCC to affect. Publishers and reporters are not alike in their ability, education, tolerance of diversity, and sense of responsibility. The hidden or overt pressures of advertisers have long been with us.

[2] From article by Nicholas Johnson, a member of the Federal Communications Commission. *Atlantic.* 221:43-51. Je. '68. Copyright © 1968, by The Atlantic Monthly Company, Boston, Mass. Reprinted with permission.

But one aspect of the problem is clearly within the purview of the FCC—the impact of *ownership* upon the content of the mass media. It is also a part of the responsibility of the Antitrust Division of the Justice Department. It has been the subject of recent congressional hearings. There are a number of significant trends in the ownership of the media worth examining—local and regional monopolies, growing concentration of control of the most profitable and powerful television stations in the major markets, broadcasting-publishing combines, and so forth. . . .

Concentration of Control Over the Media

I do not believe that most owners and managers of the mass media in the United States lack a sense of responsibility or lack tolerance for a diversity of views. I do not believe there is a small group of men who gather for breakfast every morning and decide what they will make the American people believe that day. Emotion often outruns the evidence of those who argue a conspiracy theory of propagandists' manipulation of the masses.

On the other hand, one reason evidence is so hard to come by is that the media tend to give less publicity to their own abuses than, say, to those of politicians. The media operate as a check upon other institutional power centers in our country. There is, however, no check upon the media. Just as it is a mistake to overstate the existence and potential for abuse, so, in my judgment, is it a mistake to ignore the evidence that does exist.

In 1959, for example, it was reported that officials of the Trujillo regime in the Dominican Republic had paid $750,000 to officers of the Mutual Radio Network to gain favorable propaganda disguised as news. (Ownership of the Mutual Radio Network changed hands once again last year without any review whatsoever by the FCC of old or new owners. The FCC does not regulate networks, only stations, and Mutual owns none.) RCA was once charged with using an NBC station to serve unfairly its broader corporate interests, including the coverage of RCA activities as "news," when others did not. There was speculation that after RCA acquired Random House, considerable pressure was put on the book publishing house's president, Bennett Cerf, to cease his Sunday evening service as a panelist on CBS's "What's My Line?" The Commission has occasionally found that individual stations have violated the "fairness doctrine" in advocating causes serving the station's economic self-interest, such as pay television.

Virtually every issue of the *Columbia Journalism Review* reports instances of such abuses by the print media. It has described a railroad-owned newspaper that refused to report railroad wrecks, a newspaper in debt to the Teamsters Union which gave exceedingly favorable coverage to Jimmy Hoffa, the repeated influence of the DuPont interests in the editorial functions of the Wilmington papers which it owned, and Anaconda Copper's use of its company-owned newspapers to support political candidates favorable to the company.

Edward P. Morgan left ABC last year [1967] to become the commentator on the Ford Foundation-funded Public Broadcasting Laboratory. He has always been straightforward, and he used his final news broadcast to be reflective about broadcasting itself.

Let's face it [he said]. We in this trade use this power more frequently to fix a traffic ticket or get a ticket to a ball game than to keep the doors of an open society open and swinging. . . . The freest and most profitable press in the world, every major facet of it, not only ducks but pulls its punches to save a supermarket of commercialism or shield an ugly prejudice and is putting the life of the republic in jeopardy thereby.

Economic self-interest *does* influence the content of the media, and as the media tend to fall into the control of corporate conglomerates, the areas of information and opinion affecting those economic interests become dangerously wide-ranging. What *is* happening to the ownership of American media today? What dangers does it pose? Taking a look at

the structure of the media in the United States, I am not put
at ease by what I see.

Values of Diversified Ownership

Most American communities have far less "dissemination
of information from diverse and antagonistic sources" (to
quote a famous description by the Supreme Court of the
basic aim of the First Amendment) than is available nationally. Of the 1500 cities with daily newspapers, 96 per cent are
served by single-owner monopolies. Outside the top 50 to 200
markets there is a substantial dropping off in the number of
competing radio and television signals. The FCC prohibits a
single owner from controlling two AM radio, or two television, stations with overlapping signals. But it has only
recently expressed any concern over common ownership of an
AM radio station and an FM radio station and a television
station in the same market. Indeed, such ownership is the
rule rather than the exception and probably exists in your
community. Most stations are today acquired by purchase.
And the FCC, has, in part because of congressional pressure,
rarely disapproved a purchase of a station by a newspaper.

There are few statewide or regional "monopolies"—although some situations come close. But in a majority of our
states—the least populous—there are few enough newspapers
and television stations to begin with, and they are usually
under the control of a small group. And most politicians find
today, as Congress warned in 1926, "woe be to those who dare
to differ with them." Most of our politics is still state and
local in scope. And increasingly, in many states and local
communities, congressmen and state and local officials are
compelled to regard that handful of media owners (many of
whom are out-of-state), rather than the electorate itself, as
their effective constituency. Moreover, many mass media
owners have a significant impact in more than one state. One
case that came before the FCC, for example, involved an
owner with AM-FM-TV combinations in Las Vegas and
Reno, Nevada, along with four newspapers in that state,

seven newspapers in Oklahoma, and two stations and two newspapers in Arkansas. Another involved ownership of ten stations in North Carolina and adjoining southern Virginia. You may never have heard of these owners, but I imagine the elected officials of their states return their phone calls promptly.

The principal national sources of news are the wire services, AP [Associated Press] and UPI [United Press International], and the broadcast networks. Each of the wire services serves on the order of 1200 newspapers and 3000 radio and television stations. Most local newspapers and radio stations offer little more than wire service copy as far as national and international news is concerned. To that extent one can take little heart for "diversity" from the oft-proffered statistics on proliferating radio stations (now over 6000) and the remaining daily newspapers (1700). The networks, though themselves heavily reliant upon the wire services to find out what's worth filming, are another potent force.

The weekly newsmagazine field is dominated by *Time*, *Newsweek*, and *U.S. News*. (The first two also control substantial broadcast, newspaper, and book or publishing outlets. *Time* is also in movies [MGM] and is hungry for three or four newspapers.) Thus, even though there are thousands of general and specialized periodicals and program sources with significant national or regional impact, and certainly no "monopoly" exists, it is still possible for a single individual or corporation to have vast national influence.

National Political Power

What we sometimes fail to realize, moreover, is the political significance of the fact that we have become a nation of cities. Nearly half of the American people live in the six largest states: California, New York, Illinois, Pennsylvania, Texas, and Ohio. Those states, in turn, are substantially influenced (if not politically dominated) by their major population-industrial-financial-media centers, such as Los Angeles, New York City, Chicago, and Philadelphia—the nation's four largest metropolitan areas. Thus, to have a major newspaper or television station influence in *one* of these cities is to have significant national power. And the number of interests with influence in *more* than one of these markets is startling.

Most of the top 50 television markets (which serve approximately 75 per cent of the nation's television homes) have three competing commercial VHF [Very High Frequency] television stations. There are about 150 such VHF commercial stations in these markets. Less than 10 per cent are today owned by entities that do not own other media interests. In 30 of the 50 markets at least one of the stations is owned by a major newspaper published in that market—a total of one third of these 150 stations. (In Dallas-Fort Worth *each* of the network affiliates is owned by a local newspaper, and the fourth, an unaffiliated station, is owned by Oklahoma newspapers.) Moreover, half of the newspaper-owned stations are controlled by seven groups—groups that also publish magazines as popular and diverse as *Time, Newsweek, Look, Parade, Harper's, TV Guide, Family Circle, Vogue, Good Housekeeping,* and *Popular Mechanics.* Twelve parties own more than one third of all the major-market stations.

In addition to the vast national impact of their affiliates the three television networks each own VHF stations in all of the top three markets—New York, Los Angeles, and Chicago —and each has two more in other cities in the top ten. RKO and Metromedia each own stations in both New York City and Los Angeles. Metromedia also owns stations in Washington, D.C., and California's other major city, San Francisco— as well as Philadelphia, Baltimore, Cleveland, Kansas City, and Oakland. RKO also owns stations in Boston, San Francisco, Washington, Memphis, Hartford, and Windsor, Ontario—as well as the regional Yankee Network. Westinghouse owns stations in . . . Chicago, Philadelphia *and* Pittsburgh, Pennsylvania, Boston, San Francisco, Baltimore, and Fort Wayne. These are but a few examples of today's media barons.

There are many implications of their power. Groups of stations are able to bargain with networks, advertisers, and talent in ways that put lesser stations at substantial economic disadvantage. Group ownership means, by definition, that few stations in major markets will be locally owned. (The FCC recently approved the transfer of the last available station in San Francisco to the absentee ownership of Metromedia. The only commercial station locally owned today is controlled by the San Francisco *Chronicle*.) But the basic point is simply that the national political power involved in ownership in, say, New York, Los Angeles, Philadelphia, and Washington, D.C., is greater than a democracy should unthinkingly repose in one man or corporation.

Conglomerate Corporations

For a variety of reasons, an increasing number of communications media are turning up on the organization charts of conglomerate companies. And the incredible profits generated by broadcast stations in the major markets (television broadcasters *average* a 90 to 100 per cent return on tangible investment annually) have given FCC licensees, particularly owners of multiple television stations like the networks, Metromedia, Storer Broadcasting, and others, the extra capital with which to buy the New York Yankees (CBS), Random House (RCA), or Northeast Airlines (Storer). Established or up-and-coming conglomerates regard communications acquisitions as prestigious, profitable, and often a useful or even a necessary complement to present operations and projected exploitation of technological change....

Among the national group owners of television stations are General Tire (RKO), Avco, Westinghouse, Rust Craft, Chris Craft, Kaiser and Kerr-McGee. The problem of *local* conglomerates was forcefully posed for the FCC in another case earlier this year. Howard Hughes, through Hughes Tool Company, wanted to acquire one of Las Vegas' three major television stations. He had recently acquired $125 million worth of Las Vegas real estate, including hotels, gambling casinos, and an airport. These investments supplemented 27,000 acres previously acquired. The Commission majority blithely approved the television acquisition without a hearing, overlooking FCC precedents which suggested that a closer examination was in order. In each of these instances the potential threat is ... that personal economic interests may dominate or bias otherwise independent media.

Concentration and Technological Change

The problem posed by conglomerate acquisitions of communications outlets is given a special but very important twist by the pendency of sweeping technological changes which have already begun to unsettle the structure of the industry.

President Johnson ... appointed a distinguished task force to evaluate our national communications policy and chart a course for realization of these technological promises in a manner consistent with the public interest. But private interests have already begun to implement their own plans on how to deal with the revolution in communications technology.

General Sarnoff of RCA has hailed the appearance of "the knowledge industry"—corporate casserole dishes blending radio and television stations, networks, and programing; films, movie houses, and record companies; newspaper, magazine, and book publishing; advertising agencies; sports or other entertainment companies; and teaching machines and other profitable appurtenances of the $50 billion "education biz."

And everybody's in "cable television"—networks, book publishers, newspapers. Cable television is a system for building the best TV antenna in town and then wiring it into everybody's television set—for a fee. It improves signal quality and number of channels, and has proved popular. But the new technology is such that it has broadcasters and newspaper publishers worried. For the same cable that can bring off-the-air television into the home can also bring programing from the cable operator's studio, or an electronic newspaper printed in the home by a facsimile process. Books can be delivered (between libraries, or to the home) over "television" by using the station's signal during an invisible pause. So everybody's hedging their bets—including the telephone company. Indeed, about all the vested interests can agree upon is that none of them want us to have direct, satellite-to-home radio and television. But at this point it is not at all clear who will have his hand on the switch that controls what comes to the American people over their "telephone wire" a few years hence.

What Is to Be Done?

It would be foolish to expect any extensive restructuring of the media in the United States, even if it were considered desirable. Technological change can bring change in structure, but it is as likely to be change to even greater concentration as to wider diversity. In the short run at least, economics seems to render essentially intractable such problems as local monopolies in daily newspapers, or the small number of outlets for national news through wire services, newsmagazines, and the television networks. Indeed, to a certain extent the very high technical quality of the performance rendered by these news-gathering organizations is aided by their concentration of resources into large units and the financial cushions of oligopoly profits.

Nevertheless, it seems clear to me that the risks of concentration are grave.

Chairman Philip Hart of the Senate Antitrust and Monopoly Subcommittee remarked by way of introduction to his antitrust subcommittee's recent hearings about the newspaper industry, "The products of newspapers, opinion and information, are essential to the kind of society that we undertake to make successful here." If we are serious about the kind of society we have undertaken, it is clear to me that we simply must not tolerate concentration of media ownership—except where concentration creates actual countervailing social benefits. These benefits cannot be merely speculative. They must be identifiable, demonstrable, and genuinely weighty enough to offset the dangers inherent in concentration.

This guideline is a simple prescription. The problem is to design and build machinery to fill it. And to keep the machinery from rusting and rotting. And to replace it when it becomes obsolete.

America does have available governmental machinery which is capable of scotching undue accumulations of power over the mass media, at least in theory and to some extent. The Department of Justice has authority under the antitrust laws to break up combinations which "restrain trade" or which "tend to lessen competition." These laws apply to the media as they do to any other industry.

But the antitrust laws simply do not get to where the problems are. They grant authority to block concentration only when it threatens *economic* competition in a particular economic *market*. Generally, in the case of the media, the relevant market is the market for advertising. Unfortunately, relatively vigorous advertising competition can be maintained in situations where competition in the marketplace of ideas is severely threatened. In such cases, the Justice Department has little inclination to act. . . .

Only the FCC is directly empowered to keep media ownership patterns compatible with a democracy's need for diversified sources of opinion and information.

In earlier times, the Commission took this responsibility very seriously. In 1941, the FCC ordered NBC to divest itself of one of its two radio networks (which then became ABC), barring any single network from affiliating with more than one outlet in a given city. (The Commission has recently waived this prohibition for, ironically, ABC's four new national radio networks.) In 1941 the Commission also established its power to set absolute limits on the total number of broadcast licenses any individual may hold, and to limit the number of stations any individual can operate in a particular service area.

The American people are indebted to the much maligned FCC for establishing these rules. Imagine, for example, what the structure of political power in this country might look like if two or three companies owned substantially all of the broadcast media in our major cities.

But since the New Deal generation left the command posts of the FCC, this agency has lost much of its zeal for combating concentration. Atrophy has reached so advanced a state that the public has of late witnessed the bizarre spectacle of the Justice Department, with its relatively narrow mandate, intervening in FCC proceedings, such as [the proposed merger of] ITT [International Telephone & Telegraph Corporation]-ABC, to create court cases with names like *The United States vs. the FCC.*

This history is an unhappy one on the whole. It forces one to question whether government can ever realistically be expected to sustain a vigilant posture over an industry which controls the very access of government officials themselves to the electorate.

Beyond the Reach?

I fear that we have already reached the point in this country where the media, our greatest check on other accumulations of power, may themselves be beyond the reach of any other institution: the Congress, the President, or the Federal Communications Commission, not to mention governors, mayors, state legislators, and city councilmen. Congressional hearings are begun and then quietly dropped. Whenever the FCC stirs fitfully as if in wakefulness, the broadcasting industry scurries up the Hill for a congressional bludgeon. And the fact that roughly 60 per cent of all campaign expenses go to radio and television time gives but a glimmer of the power of broadcasting in the lives of senators and congressmen. . . .

In general, I would urge the minimal standard that no accumulation of media should be permitted without a specific and convincing showing of a continuing countervailing social benefit. For no one has a higher calling in an increasingly complex free society bent on self-government than he who informs and moves the people. Personal prejudice, ignorance, social pressure, and advertiser pressure are in large measure inevitable. But a nation that has, in Learned Hand's phrase, "staked its all" upon the rational dialogue of an informed electorate simply cannot take any unnecessary risk of polluting the stream of information and opinion that sustains it. At the very least, the burden of proving the social utility of doing otherwise should be upon him who seeks the power and profit which will result.

Whatever may be the outcome, the wave of renewed interest in the impact of ownership on the role of the media in our society is healthy. All will gain from intelligent inquiry by Congress, the Executive, the regulatory commissions—and especially the academic community, the American people generally, and the media themselves. For, as the Supreme Court has noted, nothing is more important in a free society than "the widest possible dissemination of information from diverse and antagonistic sources." And if we are unwilling to discuss *this* issue fully today we may find ourselves discussing none that matter very much tomorrow.

SIX MYTHS ABOUT TELEVISION [3]

As the television network librarians begin to tally and rack this season's last cans of film and tape, it is possible to predict with sad certainty what next year will bring.

Except for more old movies, next year's commercial television will be the same as this has been. The same green tendrils of hope will grow into the same weedy crop of formula-written, formula-directed shows, ranging from pseudo-westerns through cast-iron fantasies, to what *Variety* once called hix pix. This prediction is also valid for 1968, and the year after that, and the year after that, ad infinitum.

[3] From "The Real Masters of Television," by Robert Eck, associate copy director of a Chicago advertising agency. *Harper's Magazine*. 234:45-52. Mr. '67. Copyright © 1967, by Harper's Magazine, Inc. Reprinted from the March, 1967 issue of *Harper's Magazine* by permission of the author.

Why can't commercial television be improved? After all, its diseases seem to be no mystery. Everyone knows it is infested by evil advertising men who befoul the programs with their greedy touch. Their dupes, the sponsors, are for the most part a group of well-meaning, affluent bumblers—misguided souls who need instruction in cultural responsibility from you, me, Goodman Ace, and David Susskind. The networks they deal with are stupid bureaucracies, dominated by frightened vice presidents, natural enemies of everything that is fresh and intelligent. To make matters worse, all three idiot species are being bamboozled by a fourth: the audience researcher, a charlatan who has persuaded them he can take a continuous count of the nation's many millions of television viewers, either by telephoning the homes or bugging the sets of a thousand or two families whose identities are shrouded in mystery. By contrast to these fools and villains, there are a few exemplary sponsors who, out of the sheer goodness of their enlightened hearts, pay for the programs you and I like. And waiting in the wings is a benevolent Government, needing only stronger prompting to move onstage and straighten out the mess.

If these familiar figures of cocktail-party folklore even came close to representing the actualities of commercial television, there might be some hope for improvement. But they do not. They are a collection of wishes, falsehoods, and semitruths, embodied in explanatory myths. As we shall see, it is not because of these myths but because of the more complex realities underlying them that commercial television is as amenable to reform as the adult Bengal tiger.

The Myth of the Evil Adman's Influence

While it has become fashionable among intellectual liberals to lay the sins of our materialism at the doorstep of the advertising agent, today's television programing is one sin he can rightly disclaim. He has virtually nothing to say about it. There was a time when he was a grand panjandrum of programing, but that was thirty years ago, in the heyday of radio, when advertising agencies literally produced the programs their clients sponsored. In 1940, for example, A. D. Lasker, the head of Pepsodent's advertising agency, could decide whether Bob Hope, popular star of Pepsodent's radio show, would get the thousand-dollar weekly raise he was asking for. In 1967, Johnny Carson, popular star of "The Tonight Show," who earns over $200,000 a year, need not even say hello to an advertising agent.

Although the business patterns of radio carried over into the early days of television, by the mid-1950's the television networks succeeded in taking away from the advertising men the controls they had historically exercised over program material. In this, the networks had no choice. Not only were television shows far more difficult to produce than radio shows, but television itself was rapidly growing into a business far more vast and risky—a business in which the profits (and the eventual existence of a network) depended not on its ability to cozen sponsors but to deliver measurable audience. Programing—the means of doing this—could not be left in the hands of outsiders, semiprofessionals, men to whom entertainment was only a sideline.

For the same reasons, production of television shows shifted from Chicago and New York to the foothills of the Santa Monica mountains. The moviemakers out there were not only the most expert producers of mass entertainment but also the most efficient. The money put into a live production is gone the moment the floodlights die, but films can be sold and resold, again and again, both here and abroad. A filmed TV series can be profitable even if it loses money on its first run. Nowadays, the networks make a practice of inviting advertisers and their agencies to preview the prototype films of such series (the pilots), but that's about as far as it goes. Admen do not put programs on the air, don't materially change them once they're on, and don't take them off.

The Myth of the Audience-Counting Charlatans

Nothing about television has been the subject of so much childish pique and wishful thinking as the rating services which undertake to measure television audiences. Inside the business, they are hated and feared, because their tabulations can make a man a potential millionaire or a failure in a matter of weeks. Outside, they are distrusted by many egocentric citizens who refuse to believe that the viewing habits of a small group of strangers could possibly reflect their own and, by the same token, the nation's. These are the people who, in the words of a disgusted research director, "think you have to drink the whole quart of milk to discover it is sour."

The plain truth about audience counting is that nobody in his right mind would spend millions out of a private, corporate, political, or charitable purse to propel images into an uncharted void. Even the BBC [British Broadcasting Corporation] uses random samples of its audience for guidance. And while random sampling can always be attacked because it only approaches perfection, so can a literal headcount. The more heads that must be counted, the more chances there are for human error in interviewing and arithmetic. This is why the Bureau of the Census sometimes prefers random sampling to a total count.

The standard, though far from the only audience sample in the television business is that of the Nielsen Audimeter survey, which measures audience continuously by means of a recording device attached to television sets in some 1,400 homes. There are a few drawbacks to this ingenious system. First, it assumes that whenever a set is turned on, so are its owners, which is usually, but not always, true. Second, families who are *not* keenly interested in television generally refuse to let the Nielsen people install Audimeters in their sets. Third, not all Audimeter recordings reach Nielsen headquarters in Evanston, Illinois, in time for inclusion in the tabulations. Fourth, the Nielsen sample has an admitted statistical error of three points.

Of course, the networks, the advertisers, the agencies, all of whom employ statistical experts, are fully aware of the weaknesses of the Nielsen figures; but they also know that these figures are considerably better than none at all, so they use them in a fairly uninhibited fashion.

The two most important aspects of this use seem to have escaped public notice:

(1) Both the men who run the networks and the men who run the companies that use network advertising know that everyone uses the same audience figures and that, therefore, their competitors are subject to the same errors and inadequacies as are they. For competitive business purposes, the inadequacies of the ratings tend to wash out over a period of time, just as would the inadequacies of a short deck in a poker game.

(2) The audience count is not a popularity contest or even primarily a guide to the judgment of network executives. It is part of a financial measurement.

For each dollar a businessman spends, he wants a comparative measure of what it has bought. In the case of advertising audience, his measure is cost per thousand people reached. He started using this measure long before network television, or even network radio, existed. To find which of several newspapers or magazines gave him the most for his money, he divided the cost of putting an ad in each of them by the number of thousands of people who bought copies. Now he does the same for television, dividing the cost of a minute commercial (about $40,000 in prime evening time) by the number of thousands of viewers who were tuned in. . . .

The Myth of the Bumbling, Unenlightened Sponsors

A shocking thing has happened to most old-fashioned television sponsors. They have disappeared. In their place is a heartless scheme called a scatter plan. Except in moments of extreme frustration, nobody in the business ever wanted a sponsor to vanish. A few years ago, in fact, the networks would only sell the commercial use of a weekly show to a regular weekly sponsor or, at most, to two alternating sponsors. However, the supply of companies with enough advertising money to buy television time this way is limited. NBC and CBS, then the undisputed leaders of the field, were able to attract such large advertisers without undue difficulty. But it was a different matter for ABC. Lacking the programing, the audience, and the stations to get all the large sponsors it needed, ABC began selling off its unsponsored time *à la carte,* offering smaller advertisers the chance to buy a minute here and a minute there.

What began as pure expedient has since grown to be the dominant trade practice, transformed into the scatter plan, a sophisticated purchasing device that permits the advertiser to purposefully scatter his commercials among different shows on the same network. Most television advertisers, including the biggest, are delighted with the scatter plan because it permits them to reach a wider number of viewers; it offers them more likelihood of reaching the kind of viewers they want to reach; it lets them suit their expenditures to the season (as the barrage before Christmas or June graduation indicates) ; and it averages their risks. Sponsored shows may turn out to be unwatched turkeys; scatter plans do not.

That's why probably three quarters of all national television—amounting to around a billion dollars annually—is now paid for by scatter plans. It's not unusual for Procter & Gamble, one of the country's three or four heaviest television advertisers, to have commercials for its products on thirty to forty shows. A booming pharmaceutical firm such as Miles Laboratories may have commercials on half that number. . . .

For all his arrogant foibles, the old-time sponsor usually took a proprietary pride in his show. It was more apt to be a manifestation of his vanity than an accurate reflection of the show's intrinsic worth, but it did exist and it could be appealed to. It has been replaced by the depersonalized processes of an audience market, in which viewers by the mil-

lions are counted, sorted, graded, and sold to specification
at so much a thousand head. There is not much to be gained
by writing a letter of praise—or disgust—to a scatter plan.

The Myth of the Exemplary, Enlightened Sponsors

Most of the fast-vanishing breed of real sponsors remaining on television are distinguished by their benignity. They
sponsor fine programs and regularly receive Good Boy
Medals in the forms of various trophies, plaques, and journalistic commendations, accompanied by the wistfully
spoken hope that other advertisers will take the hint and
become good boys, too.

This, alas, will never be. The good sponsor is a rare bird
not only in its sponsoring habits but also in its generally
peculiar business characteristics. Unlike the bulk of television advertisers, the sponsor of the "Bell Telephone Hour"
[now off the air] is a huge natural monopoly whose profits
will not be even slightly affected by the way it uses television.
"The Hallmark Hall of Fame" is the darling of one of the
last of the old school of owner-managers, a rough-hewn multi-
millionaire named Joyce Hall, who can do pretty much what
he likes. What he likes is to sponsor inoffensive plays of prov-
en worth, elegantly produced. The extent to which this has
helped Hallmark sales will never be known since greeting-
card sales do not respond to television advertising in the directly traceable way sales of many household products do.

Other "cultural" sponsors are often companies with small
advertising budgets who use the opportunity afforded by
public-affairs or cultural-uplift shows to buy television time
cheap. Prior to each season, the networks plan for and under-
write the costs of a number of thoughtful pieces of reportage
and a few well-intended dramatic shows, knowing even as
they do it, that low audience forecasts will make it necessary
to sell them off to commercial sponsors at a loss.

A startling insight into the strange economics of such
programs is provided by the case of the Arthur Miller play,
Death of a Salesman, one of the most impressive shows of

1966. It was produced by David Susskind and sponsored by Xerox Corporation, a company that in May 1966, received a trustees' award from the Academy of Television Arts and Sciences for its contributions to the betterment of television programing. However, Susskind was not paid to produce *Salesman* by this exemplary sponsor, but by CBS, in whose vaults the completed tape reposed for some months while CBS vainly sought sponsors—and while the asking price kept dropping. When Xerox at last bought the telecast of the play, they got it for what can be described in today's market as a song. The financial realities behind *Death of a Salesman* are:

Production cost (with no profit for the network)	$580,000
Network time charges	300,000
Total cost to CBS	$880,000
Price to Xerox	250,000
Net loss to CBS	$630,000

In other words, the real sponsor of *Death of a Salesman* was the network, which cut its losses by selling the ostensible sponsorship to Xerox, a company whose enormous profits and lack of need for broad television audience eminently qualify it for the role of patron of the arts.

As time goes by, we shall probably see fewer rather than more good sponsors in television. In the case of the authentically benevolent sponsors, the by-guess-and-by-God judgment of old-line management will give way to the facts-and-figures quantification of Harvard Business School graduates. The rest of the good sponsors are dependent on the willingness of the networks to produce and sell good shows at fire-sale prices. Since the networks' recent profits have been phenomenal, we can assume their current willingness to absorb losses for the sake of prestige is about as high as it is ever going to be. Any reverses in profit will probably be reflected by the departure of some of those good sponsors who are only good when the network helps them be.

The Myth of the Stupid Bureaucratic Networks and Their Frightened Vice Presidents

Television is a triumph of equipment over people and the minds that control it are so small you could put them in the navel of a flea and still have room beside them for a network vice president's heart.

When Fred Allen said that in 1952, he was suffering from an illusion still shared by millions who assume from the nature of most television programing that the networks are in the communications and entertainment business.

They are not. . . .

The networks' business is the audience-delivery business, and if their vice presidents are frightened men, they have good reason to be. They are involved in a unique and frightening enterprise. Their customer, the typical television advertiser, is a maker of package goods. His products (soda pop, soap, prepared foods, etc.) cost little, are bought often, and are used in every home. His audience requirements are limitless and unrelated to cultural or socioeconomic levels. He wants as much audience as he can get as cheap as he can get it.

This customer's principal audience supplier, the network, knows that for its part, the more scatter-plan audience it can deliver per dollar of production and telecasting charges, the lower the advertiser's true cost will be, the more he will tend to use the network for his advertising, and the more money the network will make. What this has led to is unparalleled in the history of publication, radio, theater, or motion pictures—a quest for audience which, carried to its logical end, is impossible and absurd. The mechanical rabbit each network is chasing is no less than total share of total audience: all the television viewers in the United States. No network will ever catch the rabbit, but they cannot stop themselves from trying.

The consequences of the chase revealed themselves drastically for the first time during the 1959-60 season, a year that give the lie to the irreparable optimists who thought, and still may think, that television, properly used, can slowly lift the tastes of the masses, show by show, until 25 million American families commonly spend evenings of Shakespeare in their living rooms.

In 1959, NBC and CBS were sufficiently rich and successful to try to inaugurate a process of cultural uplift and were, in fact, presenting a fairly wide spectrum of regular programing which ranged from "Playhouse 90" to the equally well-rehearsed "$64,000 Question." ABC, unfortunately, was poor, insecure, and ambitious. In the fall of 1959, under the guidance of a shrewd, personable sales executive, Oliver Treyz, ABC launched a group of new shows distinguished by stylized violence and unstylized gore. Its many new cops-and-robbers shows included the renowned "Untouchables" series, as well as "Hawaiian Eye" and "The Detectives," while five new westerns brought its total number of westerns to a total of ten a week.

This move was righteously criticized in press and pulpit but, in terms of the multitudes of viewers it could deliver to advertisers, the 1959-60 season proved the turning point in the fortunes of ABC. As an audience-delivery system, it suddenly moved up from a low third place to a close second, forcing NBC and CBS to compromise their programing standards so rapidly and completely that by spring of 1961, Ollie Treyz had what must have been the extreme pleasure of salting his competitors' wounds. In a speech delivered in April of that year, he accused NBC and CBS of slavishly copying ABC's grand new program ideas and coolly suggested they stick to their own lasts.

Of course they weren't about to follow Treyz's advice. He had taught them a lesson of the most unforgettable kind: an expensive one. In the audience-delivery business, you do not have the luxury of setting either your standards or those of your audience. Instead, they are set for you by the relative success of your competitors. . . .

In the circumstances, it is inaccurate to complain that the audience-delivery systems are subverting the popular taste. What they are doing is accommodating it better than it has ever been accommodated before. A prime example is the TV version of the western. Western films have been a foolproof staple of the entertainment field ever since Blace Tracey silently gunned down Silk Miller in *Hell's Hinges,* fifty years ago, because they can be filmed with cost-cutting speed and almost invariably make money. So it is hardly surprising to find a lot of television time given over to the horse opera. What comes as a slight shock is to realize that many of television's so-called westerns—including the most popular— aren't real westerns at all. From time to time, a posse may still pursue the villains up the draw, a stage may be held up, there may be gunfights; but for the most part television's western heroes are concerned with Human Problems. The badman is as frequently reformed as killed. Often he is completely missing from the script. . . .

The immense popularity of "Bonanza," champion of this new breed, testifies to the fact that the constant attempt to deliver larger audiences has made American commercial television the most awesome mechanism of mass entertainment ever devised. Week in and week out, "Bonanza" draws audiences far larger than the total population of most European countries. A number of other shows draw almost as strongly; and during the prime evening hours, the average number of viewers attracted by the combined offerings of the three networks can be estimated at around 70 million.

That is quite a house.

To suggest in the face of such monumental achievement that the networks have failed is to spit into the wind. In their own terms, at least, they have been a resounding success. Today, as they settle into their mature business practice, we can confidently expect them to continue chasing the uncatchable rabbit with the sharpened skills and elastic agility born of bitter but rewarding experience. Theirs is an infinite pursuit which has in it small room for cultural dabblings.

The Myth of the Benevolent Governmental Power

During his tenure as crusading chairman of the Federal Communications Commission, Newton Minow, with strong support from the press, managed to badger the networks into carrying slightly more public-service programing. He also managed to convey to the public the impression that the Federal Government was capable of improving the quality of commercial television.

That is mostly a false impression. Not only is the power to regulate program content specifically denied the Commission under section 326 of the Federal Communications Act; it is doubtful that any such power could exist because of the practical difficulties that lie in the way of defining it. To put up a stop sign at a traffic intersection, and require everyone to come to a full stop before crossing, is a perfectly workable arrangement. But to put up a sign saying "good judgment," and to pass a law requiring everyone to use good judgment before crossing, verges on nonsense. Yet the problem of defining good judgment at an intersection is trivial beside the problem of defining good judgment in the construction of the 7,000 hours of programing each station broadcasts in the course of a year.

What the Government can do—and has done very little— is encourage alternatives to commercial network television. With Minow cheering it on, Congress did pass a law requiring that all new TV sets be capable of receiving ultra-high-frequency signals. This was done in order to stimulate establishment of UHF stations, but whether these will ever provide an attractive alternative to the networks remains to be seen. The two UHF stations in my area fill their time with ancient, sub-B movies, sportcasts, travelogues, old BBC programs, and the Manion Forum. . . .

Again, by encouraging that fifteen-year-old orphan, pay-TV, the FCC might help create a desirable alternative to present commercial programing. A year ago, after studying the 1965 petition of Zenith Radio Corporation—which, with RKO General, has been running a long-term pay-TV experiment in Hartford, Connecticut—the Commission declared itself ready to authorize national pay-TV, subject to comment from those affected by it. At this writing, it had not acted, but favorable action was expected.

The common denominator of these alternatives is that all of them—UHF, satellite communications, pay-TV—are products of advances in a sophisticated and rapidly accelerating technology. This technology itself eventually may supply the most flexible and practical alternative to commercial television in the form of a simple, low-cost video recorder-player for home use. There now exists a small recorder which uses ordinary quarter-inch audio tape to record and play back color and black-and-white television programs. Invented by Marvin Camras of the Illinois Institute of Technology's Research Institute, it is capable of recording or playing two hours of unbroken material and could be made to sell for less than $300. In essence, the video recorder (and someday there will be even easier and cheaper forms of it) is an alternative not only to commercial television, but also to pay-TV, for widespread ownership of recorders would result in a video recording industry and in the sale, rental, and library loan of recorded television programs of much the same general range as today's audio recordings. The effective differences between commercial television, pay-TV, and video recording can be put this way: no matter how much you might like to see a special television production of *Der Freischütz*, you are not likely to see it on commercial television. In the improbable event that it does appear, it will do so just once, on a Saturday or Sunday afternoon, and it will be thoroughly fractured by commercials. Your chances of seeing it on pay-TV would probably not be a great deal better. If it should be programed, there would be no commercials, but you would have to watch it on one of the few days it was being presented. With video recorders and recordings, your chances of seeing *Der Freischütz* would be quite good. You could rent it without any commercials and watch it any time of the day you pleased.

The Fault Lies in the System

Unfortunately, however, this agreeable prospect lies some distance in the future—by five, ten, or fifteen years. Right now, the large electronic firms are too busy making color sets for the multitudinous majority who dote on commercial television to worry about making recorders for the minority who do not.

And until video recording or some other alternative is realized, we will continue to be stuck with commercial television, which will continue to grind its repetitive, skillful, profitable way. Television reviewers will angrily scold, instructively praise, and loudly hope. Television producers will brag about hairbreadth advances over mediocrity. Television executives will count their cultural contributions and discuss their frequently magnificent public-information programs. Do not be deceived. Critics and defenders alike are symbiotically linked to the great audience-delivery systems. Those systems are married to cost-per-thousand, compelled to the pursuit of total audience, and—with factories in Hollywood, main offices in New York, gala introductory promotions each fall, and franchised dealers throughout the country—are among America's biggest and most successful mass-production businesses.

A CRITIQUE OF TV NEWSCASTING [4]

Television's most impressive and predictable spectacle is the coverage of election night. In one generation TV has transformed the anxious, all-night ritual into an incredible

[4] From "The News on TV and How It Is Unmade," adapted from *The People Machine* by Robert MacNeil. Copyright © 1968 by Robert MacNeil. Originally appeared in *Harper's Magazine,* and reprinted by permission of Harper & Row, Publishers. Text from *Harper's Magazine.* 237:72-80. O. '68. Robert MacNeil is a reporter for the BBC in London and a former New York TV journalist.

display of electronic virtuosity. It has dazzled, and not always pleased, the voters with its ability to tell them who won, before some voters have even gone to the polls. The public is still mystified and a little annoyed that there is no longer any "horse race." There never was, of course, except in very close elections. Old-fashioned reporting techniques merely created that pleasurable illusion.

Illusions of a different sort are created by TV. For its journalists are enmeshed in a system that looks upon news as another commodity, which sells or does not sell, attracts audiences or does not, which—like other commodities—can be shaped, reworked, and manipulated, or simply dropped. There is, however, one factor that distinguishes news from almost everything else the networks transmit: prestige.

Thus, for example, on June 14, 1967, NBC's local station in New York published an advertisement in the New York *Times* to promote the "Eleventh Hour News" and its anchorman, Jim Hartz. The program had earned considerable public following in several years of competent reporting but that wasn't good enough for the PR men. "Jim and the Eleventh Hour Staff pore over thousands of reports compiled each day by NBC News correspondents in seventy-five countries to bring you New York's most meaningful late-evening report," the advertisement said.

It is true that NBC News employs a large staff in the United States and up to a dozen correspondents overseas. But they do not compile "thousands of reports" each day; they compile very few. As do the other networks, NBC bases the bulk of its news service on the worldwide facilities of the Associated Press, United Press International, and Reuters. The networks also have interlocking arrangements to exchange news film made by other broadcasting organizations. On occasion, the services of "stringers" or part-time correspondents employed by a newspaper or wire service are called upon, though more often for radio than for television. At the particular period of the advertisement quoted, in fact, WNBC had introduced an economy wave. The budget of the "Eleventh Hour News" did not permit it to pay for as many fresh reports from around the United States each evening as it had customarily used, so there was less "poring" than usual. . . .

The "Star System" for TV News

The chief difference between television and newspaper journalism lies in their respective attitudes to the function of the reporter. Television news has not found a central role for the reporter. Preoccupation with the logistical problems of getting "picture" have made the TV reporter secondary, while show-business economics have replaced him in the studio with a "commentator" or front man.

Entertainment TV disposes the audience to be attracted by personable stars. Viewers develop their loyalties and habits by identifying particular programs with particular stars. From the beginning, the industry handled news in the same way. Huge audiences for news grew as star commentators became centerpieces. It has proved so difficult to fit reporters into this pattern that they often have been reduced to a form of window dressing.

The incentives of success are also different from those in print journalism, for the system of rewards belongs to the entertainment industry. During a strike in April 1967 by the television artists' union (AFTRA), Chet Huntley complained that it was demeaning for journalists to be members of a union of "singers, actors, jugglers, announcers, entertainers, and comedians." Demeaning or not, it has a certain logic because TV newsmen are paid in the same manner as singers, actors, and comedians—by the appearance. With some recent exceptions, network newsmen make their money from fees paid on top of a basic salary.

Reporters contributing to television news shows receive fees ranging from $25 to $150 for each item used on a program containing commercials. A man may spend three or four days quietly digging for facts to support a story, only to find himself receiving a fee of $50 if his story is used—or nothing if the story does not pan out. His colleague, meanwhile, may use the same amount of time rushing to snatch an interview here and put together a few superficial facts there, may place ten separate pieces on the air, and may as a result pocket $500. Obviously the system discourages methodical pursuit of information. The object is to get each story on the air and move on to something else.

What a "Star" Reflects

The commentator is the pinnacle of a system which glorifies him at the expense of the reporter. Once the broadcast journalist has made the grade and is found to have attributes desirable on the screen, he is rewarded by being taken out of the field. He is given regular commitments as anchorman on one or another regularly scheduled program. A commentator presenting a five-minute daily television news program on the network receives an additional $400 a week. Preparing and broadcasting a five-minute radio news program once a day for five days a week pays $250. Fees for longer news programs are negotiable, and because they are paid in the manner of show-business personalities, network newsmen find it necessary to hire agents to bargain for them with the employers. For commentators who are much in demand, annual incomes of $50,000 to $80,000 are common at the network level. For the biggest stars, such as Huntley, Brinkley, and Cronkite, the figures are much higher. . . .

To put it in its worst light, the work of the commentator is a form of parasitic journalism. He either rewrites the news from the wire services or, depending on the importance of the program and the magnitude of his stardom, he has a team of writers to do it for him. It is as though the rewrite man on a newspaper were elevated to the salary and prominence of a managing editor, and his byline placed over most of the stories.

Those who remain in the field as reporters, either by professional choice or because the networks did not think them star material, can be frustrated men. For example, the NBC

London correspondent may attend a briefing at 10 Downing Street with the press secretary of the Prime Minister. Yet he will not be the one who tells Americans about it. Chet Huntley will do it. What Huntley says, in all probability, will not even be taken from the notes of the NBC correspondent, but from the notes of the AP or UPI reporter who also covered the briefing with him. Only if the whim strikes the producer of the "Huntley-Brinkley Report" will NBC's own correspondent report from London, either very expensively by satellite, or, with a day's delay, on film. . . .

The reason for this basic shortcoming of TV journalism —its neglect of the true reporting function—is partly economic; but it also stems from a particular view of the news. Walter Scott, the NBC board chairman, whose public utterances are remarkably unpretentious for a network executive, has said

Because television *is* a visual medium, it may scant the background and significance of events to focus on the outward appearance—the comings and goings of statesmen instead of the issue that confronts them.

The comings and goings make easy pictures; the issues usually do not. Obviously, most of the energy and organization of television goes into getting pictures. The logistics of doing that are so formidable (and so expensive) that they overshadow everything else. Consequently, from its inception television news has been criticized for a tendency to let pictures dictate the story. Television newsmen cannot be blamed for wanting to put visual material on a visual medium, but when this preoccupation overrides news judgment, it encourages emphasis on action rather than on significance and the playing up of trivial or exciting occurrences simply because they can be covered by cameras. That has been the burden of complaint about TV's vivid, and often heroic, coverage of the Vietnam war.

Shooting "Bloody" in Vietnam

By the end of 1967, NBC and CBS were each reported to be spending two million dollars a year on covering the

Vietnam war, and ABC, one million. Each network maintained a staff of two dozen or more people in Saigon and the film shot in jungle battles had appeared prominently on the news programs virtually every night for two years. Much was written about "the first television war" and the probable political effects of having a war which so divided the nation brought so vividly into American homes. No one is certain what that effect has been. Morris Janowitz, a University of Chicago sociologist, has said that television coverage had "hardened and polarized public sentiment." He added, "Those people who are skeptical of the war now have a vehemence in their skepticism. Those who are for the war see Americans being killed and they don't want those sacrifices to be in vain." Other observers have echoed that view.

Another point of view suggests itself, however, if the nature of television's coverage is considered. Overwhelmingly, what has been seen on the home screen has been battle action. Camera teams and reporters in Vietnam found that no matter what they filmed, the networks wanted action footage. At CBS, Vietnam hands used the expression "shooting bloody" to describe the filming they had to do to get on the air. It was not that they were ordered to shoot only war scenes, but when they shot a political story or the progress of the pacification program as well as war scenes, it would be the action film which the program producers selected. Night after night for two years, American families have seen badly wounded Americans, sacks of dead Americans being loaded for shipment home, sprawled heaps of small, dead Vietnamese bodies. There are those who believe that this portrayal of horror has sickened Americans and turned many against the war, which has seemed increasingly pointless. Yet the horror has been heavily edited, and that may also have had a political impact. By exposing the mass audience to more vivid and horrible battle events than have ever been brought into American homes before, but by cutting out what is most unbearable, it may be that television has built up a tolerance for the frightful, a feeling that war really is bearable. The grisly truth has been shown in the screening rooms of the network news departments. There would be close-up footage, with sound, of a young soldier, whose leg had been shot away a moment before, screaming obscenities at the medics, pleading with them in desperation to stop his agony. As someone who believed before 1964 that this war was a futile and stupid waste of American energies, I often wondered as I watched this uncut footage at NBC whether we should not be putting on even more of the horror, so as to arouse people more. We did not because, as one man put it, and not facetiously, "We go on the air at suppertime." ...

It is also possible that because audiences have been conditioned to the staged violence of television serials the emotional impact of the Vietnam footage has been diminished. Real violence often seems curiously tame and insignificant compared with fictional horrors. It was remarked at the time that Lee Harvey Oswald's shooting by Jack Ruby, as carried by TV, looked amateurish; the action occurred too quickly, there was no buildup.

All these factors have helped dilute the impact of the nightly war coverage. It was not until the sudden reverses of the Tet offensive in February 1968 that a majority of Americans seemed decisively moved by events of the war. Then television appeared to be moving with public opinion rather than leading or molding it.

Until the Tet offensive raised the rate of American deaths to over five hundred a week, television had not treated the story as a crisis or a national emergency. There were a few attempts at longer treatments of the political and economic issues, but for the most part not when a majority of the television audience was around. NBC ran a "Vietnam Weekly Review" for over a year at midafternoon on Sundays, but finally took it off in 1967 when no sponsors could be interested. The program was hastily resurrected after Tet. "ABC Scope" was a weekly series of half-hour programs, also run at odd weekend hours, and discontinued for financial reasons in January 1968. Though the United States was by then engaged in a major war, the nation's most important news medium was not even reviewing the war week by week.

It is interesting to consider what effect there might have been on the Administration if one network had decided that the war needed greatly expanded coverage and deserved at least one hour of prime time on a weekday evening. Assuming that the other networks would have followed suit, the impact might have been very great. For example, Morley Safer's piece on the Marines in Vietnam (CBS-TV) showed Marines setting fire to the huts in a village with cigarette lighters, and infuriated the Pentagon. Defense Department officials tried to pressure CBS into removing Safer, who is a Canadian, from Vietnam. Perhaps it is significant that the one piece of television war reporting which notoriously went against the grain of the Pentagon appeared on a network which had no affiliations with large defense contractors.

Stealthy Cheerleaders

The Vietnam war obviously presented the television networks with a dilemma. It is the best and most exciting story going and therefore merits vivid coverage. At the same time it has seriously divided the country. The industry has reacted in a manner that is now habitual: it has covered the action, done a minimum of explaining, and taken no moral stand until very late in the day. One wonders how television would have treated the Second World War. Presumably because the nation was almost unanimous in support of the President's policy, television would have acted as a cheerleader for the country. That is closer to the natural inclinations of the industry than frosty detachment. Thin bits of cheerleading can be heard through the coverage of the Vietnam war. . . .

If a commentator wishes, he can make his attitude known in a multitude of subtle ways by varying his expression or intonation. More important, however, are the facts the commentator chooses to use and the form of words used to report them. In a situation like the Vietnam story, which appears night after night, it is possible consistently to accentuate the positive elements in the news and to give less emphasis to the negative. Simply by beginning each story with the American initiative that day and the number of Vietcong reported killed, you can create a sense of American achievement and progress. By beginning your story with an account of the enemy's initiative, you convey the opposite impression. This is putting it crudely, and I am not imputing to all well-known TV commentators a deliberate attempt to slant the news. Personal attitudes and emotions are a factor in how a story is told.

My complaint is that it took television so long to tell the American people frankly how disastrously the war was going. By the time the industry did, and then almost to a man, in February 1968, the evidence was so overwhelming that a good proportion of the public had made up its mind anyway.

The Vietnam war is a good case over which to argue the morality of television's refusal to take an editorial position. It is true that some stations do present editorials, chiefly on local issues. The networks do not, but it is time they did. What tended to happen, at least over Vietnam, was that stealthy editorializing in support of the Administration slipped through, but criticism did not. There was implied cheerleading in the nightly preoccupation with battles and body counts and often cursory treatment of congressional debate.

The Reassurance Syndrome

Television journalism often appears anxious to sell the chief commodity of entertainment TV—reassurance. Apart from a tone of somewhat deeper unction on occasions of sadness, as during coverage of Martin Luther King's or Robert Kennedy's assassination, the heavily stylized mode of delivery—half sung, half chanted—of many news broadcasters makes most of the stories sound alike and imparts a certain artificiality to the content. That, coupled with the tendency of newscasters to punctuate their performances with smiles, conveys a false geniality which drains the news of meaning.

Research into audience preferences in New York and Los Angeles has revealed that newscasters who could reduce the anxiety level of audiences and present the news in a context of reassurance had tremendous appeal. The most successful personalities on the air were those who could take the edge off what was unpleasant. . . .

The television news departments offer what sounds like a respectable defense for their avoidance of controversial stands. They operate under the restraints of FCC regulations, which require them to present both sides on matters of controversy. When they do examine controversial matters they are fair to the point of irresponsibility. William S. Paley, defending Edward R. Murrow's broadcast on Senator Joseph McCarthy in 1954, said that fairness cannot be reduced to a mathematical formula. He went on

And it must be recognized that there is a difference between men, ideas, and institutions: some are good and some are bad, and it is up to us to know that difference—to know what will hold up democracy and what will undermine it—and then not to do the latter.

That was powerful stuff in 1954. It would be today. Unfortunately, today only the critics complain about the absurdity of mathematical fairness, not the broadcasters. Indeed, one gets the impression that they prefer to use the Fairness Doctrine as a shield rather than as a weapon. . . .

It is difficult to believe that it is fear of Government regulation which keeps broadcasting so sterile of opinion. Government regulation by the FCC does not appear to be nearly so effective in bringing broadcasters to heel as is the occasional direct interference of an elected official or the general awareness of being part of a business community with a large stake in the economy.

All this has a particular relevance to politics. If the nation's chief medium of journalism is suffused with show-business values; if it does not regard digging for facts as its primary function and subordinates the reporter's role; if it concentrates on recording action rather than probing significance; if it fails to analyze the news for fear of being dull or of dipping into controversy, then television journalism is not fulfilling the traditional journalistic role of putting public men and their activities under the kind of scrutiny that will provide a public check to their actions.

IN DEFENSE OF TV JOURNALISM [5]

If television reporting can avoid serious Government interference for one more generation, it will be home free. But first those who want to establish controls must die off— my generation and yours if, just to pick a shibboleth, you remember the Korean War directly or from newspapers rather than from history books. On the younger side of that divide people tend to accept television reporting: They like it, dislike it or ignore it, but they do not blame it for causing the conditions it shows. For them it has always been there, like running water in kitchens and "psychedelic" lights at high school dances.

Your generation and mine knew journalism without television, however, and in a perfect example of *post hoc ergo propter hoc* [after this, therefore because of this] illogic we blame television's methods of reporting the news, and the fact that it does, for what we do not understand or do not care to live with. The two major news stories in our day are both dramatically of this kind: the war in Vietnam and racial disorders in the cities. And never has there been such a time for exhorting a news medium to help solve the problem, for insisting that it submerge itself in self-policing methods, for suggesting that it be controlled by law and administrators.

[5] From "The Case for TV Journalism," by Reuven Frank, executive vice president of NBC News. *New Leader.* 51:18-20. Mr. 25, '68. Reprinted from *The New Leader* of March 25, 1968. Copyright © 1968 The American Labor Conference on International Affairs. Inc.

Whose Ox Is Gored?

When news outlets are criticized in sober, general, theoretical terms for alleged involvement in situations of major
social concern, the criticism can often be traced specifically
to whoever's ox is being gored. All editors know this, and use
such devices as a "letters to the editor" column as lightning
rod and circulation builder, while pretending to discharge
their putative obligation to be balanced. But television has
no practical way to use this approach, so we TV journalists
are left with a field of gored oxen and admonitions to change
our ways. Sometimes the threat of control is stated openly,
sometimes it is only implied.

Our post-Korean young think of television, including
television news, as part of the Establishment. The Establishment does not. There are military men who tell us it is how
we are reporting the Vietnam war that is causing all those
doubts. Arthur Sylvester, the Defense Department's former
press spokesman, used to make speeches in public about how
our film concentrates on specific occurrences without showing what is going on simultaneously to the right and the left.
Several weeks ago, in Saigon, a Marine colonel told me our
reporters were so harried by our deadline conditions that
they could not place specific events in the context of larger
military objectives. Perhaps we should require our reporters
to hold up each story twenty-four hours so they could gather
perspective, he suggested; perhaps commanding officers
should insist on it. Then he asked what degree of strategic
expertise we required of reporters before assigning them to
cover the war.

Gored oxen. Many generals taste frustration because
there is less national and emotional support than they would
like for the way the war is going, even among the majority
that backs the war itself. And it is a cliché by now that Marines never think they are getting a good enough press.

Sooner or later the criticism falls into this pattern: (1)
yes, television is telling the truth; but (2) it is not telling
the whole truth; and (3) if the whole truth were told our

(the critics') positions would be the popular ones. The critic never concedes he is advocating that we manipulate the audience for him.

Generals and civilians who direct the military are men under self-control, and their argument rarely becomes shrill. In Vietnam itself, reporters from all media have benefited from a degree of cooperation known in no other war. While some young firebrands on the scene complain about restrictions, veteran war correspondents are awestruck at how much help is available. There is certainly more understanding and more intelligent help in the mechanics and logistics of getting the news out. Lately, too, the military's unhappiness with television news has been subdued and lingers only in the background, like a toothache.

Covering the Urban Riots

In the case of urban riots, the situation is quite different. Here the demands are many, the chorus is swelling, and the issue is acute. The owner of this gored ox is the white middle-class majority: well-meaning, self-congratulating, suddenly offended, and frightened. Late in the summer of 1967, NBC News sent a memorandum to all its staff members which began:

It seems that honest, intelligent people, some of them in positions of authority, are ready and willing to impose controls on television news coverage and presentation. The reason is the perhaps natural confusion of a news medium with the information it carries. This information may be unpleasant, unpalatable, and disturbing. Those who are disturbed will always accuse the medium of creating the disturbance it reports. It's happened to other media. It's our turn.

Let us recognize that the vulnerability of this medium to control is greater than that of other media. This is not a matter of debate; this is a matter of law. These controls are somehow imposed on the fallacious ground that an evil unreported would thus be an evil prevented; in this instance, at this time of history, control of television news would be presumed by the controllers to prevent or ameliorate race rioting. It must be assumed that these controls once imposed would not be limited to this subject or this field of human activity. We believe that the principal loser would be the American audience, but the control would be exercised against television news.

The memorandum went on to cite a serious instance of alleged misconduct for which the network was being criticized publicly as well as privately in high places. According to a story in the Washington Sunday *Star* of August 6, 1967, an NBC television newsman had stated that civil rights demonstrators in Cambridge, Maryland, conferred with assembled broadcast cameramen and then agreed to move scheduled demonstrations back from 8 P.M. to 6 P.M. so that the camerman would have time to fly their film to New York for the 11 P.M. news roundups. "Yet the public was given the impression that they were seeing largely 'spontaneous crowds of protesters,' " the paper charged.

After investigating the allegations, NBC found that the article was written by a "freelance writer who had no direct knowledge of the event." Moreover, the network memorandum continued, "All men on the scene told us no such thing happened, that the 8 P.M. meeting in fact took place at 9:30 P.M. rather than at 6 P.M.

When NBC called the author of the story to ask where he got his information, he said he was not referring to the Cambridge rally of July 24, 1967, which had ended in a riot; he was referring to demonstrations two or three years earlier in the same city that had nothing to do with black power and did not end in a riot. Nowhere in his article, though, was there any indication that the author meant anything but July 24, 1967, and people honestly concerned about the rioting on that day eagerly blamed the TV crews because of the newspaper story.

Blaming TV for Society's Ills

Great damage has been done to us and to our profession by these false and misleading statements [NBC concluded]. Steps are being taken to secure a retraction, but it will never catch up. The atmosphere of frustration engendered by this summer's riots is expressing itself in a need to lash out at television reporting. Nor do we believe that such actions, if taken, would be unpopular. We can expect that Americans . . . will soon believe that NBC rigged the riots in Cambridge, Maryland.

In fact, no evidence could be found that the TV newsmen had rigged anything on any date. The author of the *Star* article, a staff employee of a Senate committee, had gotten his information from the author of another article, who claimed to have gotten his information from a former NBC News staff member.

But the incident is not an isolated phenomenon. There have been statements by senators, congressmen, mayors, police directors and editorial writers claiming that the riots in the cities were caused, or at least exacerbated, by what the rioters saw on television. In his article on "Mass Media and Mass Violence" in the *New Leader* of January 15, Eugene Methvin, an associate of *Reader's Digest,* cited to this effect Senator Hugh Scott of Pennsylvania, Mayor Richard Daley of Chicago, the police director of Newark, an editor of the Detroit *News,* and supported their view (or were they supporting his?). Somehow, he did not quote Representative Durward Hall (Republican, Missouri), who told Congress on July 27, 1967:

National commentators on television and radio decry what is happening today, but over many yesterdays they permitted their facilities to be used as incitement to riot—and now they too are reaping what they have sowed.

How many times have Stokely Carmichael and like figures been on "Meet the Press," "The Today Show," "Huntley-Brinkley," and countless other channels of national communication? How many times have the major networks permitted a Carmichael or a "Rap" Brown to use their facilities to enter the homes of millions of Americans with their messages of hate and violence?

A Stokely Carmichael calling for insurrection on a street corner soap box is a curiosity—a "hippie" talking to a few other "hippies." But a Stokely Carmichael talking face to face to millions of people, recognized by those whose responsibility it is to make sober judgment about whom to give mass exposure, is immediately transformed from an oddball to a national figure. How else did a King—Martin Luther—receive international acclaim and a prize from a dynamiter's rationalization? . . .

Since Methvin further omitted the mayor of Plainfield, New Jersey—who told congressmen that rioting in his city was caused by ghetto dwellers sitting before their television screens and watching the people in Newark loot with impunity—perhaps he knows enough about Newark and Plainfield to know that communication between those two cities, and especially between their ghettos, needed no help from television. Nor did he quote Roger Wilkins, director of the Community Relations Service of the Department of Justice. Wilkins told the President's National Advisory Commission on Civil Disorders that a Department of Justice study in more than two hundred cities—some the scenes of big riots, others of little riots, and most of no riots at all—had found no evidence that rioting resulted from or was even encouraged by riots being reported on television.

The "Propagating Effect" of TV News

I don't want to pick on Methvin. He simply said what a lot of people are saying. The President's Commission on Civil Disorders recently held a special weekend for representatives of news media, with one session for the pencil and print fellows and one for TV men. Commissioners divided their time between the two groups. Several of the participants tell me the meetings with the newspaper and magazine group were about improving coverage. The TV meetings kept coming back to whether our coverage had in any way been responsible for what happened. One staff member used the words "propagating effect"—which has such a nicety of phrasing, such an implication of social insight, that I fear the fact that no direct evidence has been adduced to support it will not be enough to drive it away.

Methvin also reflected the feelings of many people when he said: "The journalists' own freedom will diminish or grow in direct proportion to the public's confidence in their performance." I submit that this mild-sounding orotundity is a blatant and dangerous misreading of the history of the American free press and of its role in American society. This is the kind of statement American correspondents hear from Foreign Office secretariats, and not only in Communist countries.

Now we hear it at home. One can only guess at the reasons. The obvious guess is blaming the messenger for the message; the Persians used to execute couriers who brought bad news. I suggest that an even better guess is the reluctance (it should be a refusal) of television journalists to help achieve the often noble aims of their critics—in other words to be conscious instrumentalities of social control.

If television in truth caused the riots, then rats and unemployment and hopelessness did not. Regardless of whether those who accuse TV think this is what they are saying, those who agree with them think it is. I have little doubt that restrictions on television reporting, motivated as punishment but rationalized as social uplift, would be popular in some Government circles and in most of middle-class white America. If the public's confidence in what we are doing is undermined, with more or less conscious intent, it is true that our freedom will be diminished. The law makes it possible; there is an atmosphere abroad which makes it thinkable.

I don't know about other people's intellectual friends, but mine want mankind to be free in order to achieve their own aims, and to find happiness in the society they envisage. Their criticism of television's performance usually winnows down to criticism of television for being invented. Almost as often, criticism of television journalism for too little coverage develops into criticism of TV for reporting too much. Both these observations apply to people who complain of shortcomings in the coverage of the two current major news stories. There should be less reporting, they argue, and more background, more analysis, or interpretation, or whatever the word is. The assumption is that background, analysis, etc. will help bring about the conditions that these honest men honestly believe will be better for us all.

What Kind of Journalism?

But the proper business of journalism is journalism. The First Amendment was written by men who believed government should be checked, and that free journalism—not necessarily responsible journalism, not specifically socially useful journalism, not exclusively ethically directed journalism—was a good check. This may seem like a witless way to do business. Yet between one time and another in history, between one country and another across the face of the earth, the consensus varies concerning the better society journalism should foster. Whose word is to be taken about what should be done?

In the late fifties we television journalists were accused of helping achieve a racially integrated society. We were not consciously boosting integration or anything else, but those who opposed what was happening blamed television news for it. Others, especially in the North, applauded the aim and refrained from criticism, not because they recognized we were not responsible for social change but because they approved of what they thought we were doing.

Today there are serious students, particularly among Negroes, who think integration cannot be effective as a first step. The upgrading of ghetto residents must precede. If the law a few years back could have forced television reporting to help (or hinder) the process of integration, would that still look like such a good idea today? But the law would already be in force. Television reporting could be required to take part in projects noble in concept but not journalistic. The access of the American public to free information would end up controlled, limited, directed.

Reporters have one thing in common with minorities: In time, history judges a society not only on what it does to them but on what it does to itself thereby.

IV. WHAT FUTURE FOR MASS COMMUNICATIONS?

EDITOR'S INTRODUCTION

The two articles that comprise this section are offered as food for thought about the future of mass communications in America and the world. After reading them, no one will doubt that we are in for some amazing developments. Yet, even as science goes forward, the problems of content remain. In tomorrow's world, when men can reach each other across the world at the touch of a fingertip, what will be the content of their expression?

The first article in this section, taken from the late, lamented *Saturday Evening Post,* describes "Tomorrow's Many-Splendored Tune-In" for television. Even today television has become the dominant medium of our time. Tomorrow? With its possibilities for pay TV, for one hundred or more programs via cable TV, for even do-it-yourself TV—tomorrow may see television playing an even more profound role in our lives.

The last article of this compilation explores, as it should, the future of worldwide communications. With the likely advent of worldwide television and other forms of instantaneous communication among peoples in all parts of the globe, these are some of the prospects in store: a narrowing of the so-called technological gap among advanced, industrial nations through the worldwide sharing of scientific and other information; a speeding up of the development process in Asia, Africa, and Latin America; greater contacts with Eastern Europe and the Soviet Union; and a strengthening of American society through more efficient transmission and storage of information from abroad.

The world of the future will be more dependent on mass communications than ever before. Will the media—private and public—rise to meet the challenges and the opportunities?

TOMORROW'S MANY-SPLENDORED TUNE-IN? [1]

"The television set of the future will be an information center, order-processing center and communications center for the home," says George Mansour, manager of TV products for Motorola, without the slightest mention of a "might" or a "probably."

While TV viewers in the fall of 1968 are sinking into their nightly soporific of situation comedies and escapist adventure shows, engineers are developing technology that will make the visual displays about the "Star Trek" spaceship Enterprise look like a nickelodeon. They are working to expand the role of the TV set far beyond its present use as an entertainment appliance; eventually it may become the electronic heart of the average home, dispensing a wide range of goods and services.

Surprisingly, this technology is not very many breakthroughs away. With a few important exceptions, scientists have already solved the theoretical problems and made the major breakthroughs required to produce any TV hardware broadcasters might conceivably need in the last quarter of the century. "For a few million dollars," says James Hillier, RCA's vice president for research, "we could build right now a television system with an eight-foot picture. It would have the quality of a travel poster and a three-dimensional effect besides."

"The future of television is no longer a question of what we can invent," says Commissioner Nicholas Johnson of the Federal Communications Commission. "It is a question of what we want."

[1] From article by Sandford Brown, formerly a contributing writer for the *Saturday Evening Post*. *Saturday Evening Post*. 241:38-9+. N. 30. '68. Reprinted by permission.

Drastic Change in the Offing

What *do* we want?

We are not, as a matter of fact, really sure. It is character-istic of the twentieth century that our technology outraces our ability to assimilate it. Which of the many television delights now being prepared in laboratories we will actually experience—or whether there will simply be megadeaths of boredom by mass stupefaction—depends on economic, poli-tical and esthetic imponderables that are almost beyond predicting. Acutely aware that drastic change is in the offing and that its own existence could be at stake, the communi-cations industry is engaged in massive maneuvering for strategic position.

The presumed guardian of the public interest, the United States Government, is the biggest imponderable of all. It is supposed to regulate the use of the electromagnetic spectrum with the long-range benefits to society in mind, but actually it does nothing of the sort. There is, in fact, a giant lack of anything resembling a logical, coherent plan. The Federal Communications Commission normally assumes a passive judicial role, arbitrating disputes among competing eco-nomic interests in a random, unplanned way. Says Nicholas Johnson, an articulate, young (thirty-four) Washington law-yer who is a frequent dissenter from FCC decisions, "We really have no sense of where we're going." [See Commis-sioner Johnson's views in "The Media Barons and the Pub-lic Interest," in Section III, above.]

The most assimilable changes involving the least uncom-fortable wrenchings of the status quo will be those involving the TV tube itself. All sets in the not distant future will be color instruments, with black-and-white having long before gone the way of the windup phonograph. Battery-operated sets will be as common as transistor radios are today, and many homes will have a TV set in every room, or perhaps display devices piping off a central receiver. The general use of integrated circuits and "modular construction" will make sets smaller, simpler, more reliable and less expensive, and may forever loosen the TV repairman's grip on the U.S. economy. When something goes wrong, the set owner need only have the repairman stop by to see which module, or section of circuitry, is causing the trouble, and replace it with a new module on the spot.

Smaller sets do not, of course, mean smaller screens. The aim will always be to increase the size of the picture. TV engineers expect screens to get much bigger, but the real problem, as one industry man puts it, is "breaking out of the bottle." The one part of a TV set that cannot be miniaturized is the cathode-ray picture tube, which produces the TV picture by beaming a stream of electrodes against a phosphor screen. Tubes have been progressively shortened relative to screen area to make TV sets flatter, but this process has gone about as far as it can.

Some attempts are being made to broaden the beam's projection by various reflective techniques. But the ultimate screen, says Christopher Carver, GE's planning manager for visual communication, will translate the TV signal into a visual display without a cathode-ray tube. However, this is probably "ten years away from even a laboratory prototype." The trouble is that the TV signal would have to be converted into an image at the screen, requiring a separate circuit for each of thousands of points on the screen analogous to the tiny phosphors in present receivers. But rough approximations of the screen of the future have been assembled in laboratories. Some use light-emitting diodes or electroluminescent panels embedded in the screen; perhaps the most interesting variation is an RCA receiver that emits no light at all but forms the TV picture on "liquid crystal" by reflecting the light from its surroundings. But nothing like a commercially acceptable picture has yet been produced, for this would require 300,000 circuits to carry the TV signal to the screen. RCA's screen, for reasons of cost, uses only a few hundred diodes.

Three-dimensional TV is even farther away, if it is coming at all. The two most promising methods involve "lenticular" screens of two separate images and various holographic techniques, but they would add enormously to the transmitting problem, requiring a signal that carried roughly thirty times the amount of information needed for a standard two-dimensional TV picture. There is some doubt that the public would be eager to pay for it, in view of the fairly tepid reception given to 3-D movies. However, one network is convinced 3-D will be much more important in TV simply because "television is more connected with reality." The re-creation of reality in the living room—from a visual and auditory if not a programing standpoint—is, of course, the goal toward which everyone is striving.

Prospects for Cable TV

A much more disruptive bit of scientific achievement, already causing quite a bit of havoc, is community antenna television (CATV) or, more popularly now, cable TV. The basic idea is simple: To improve TV reception, especially in fringe areas, very tall central antennas are built. For a monthly fee, homes are connected to the system with a coaxial cable. The subscriber not only receives much improved reception but is able to pick up many stations totally beyond the range of his home antenna. Cable viewers are still only a small segment of the total TV audience—there are about 3.5 million homes hooked up—but a CATV building boom has been underway for a decade and there are moves to bring the service into cities where reception is often blurred and distorted by tall buildings.

The implications of CATV are more complex. Almost everyone now agrees that over-the-air broadcasting direct to home antennas is going to be phased out and that all television will eventually be CATV. The nation will be dominated by several hundred local CATV systems that will be interconnected by microwave "wave guides," or even laser beams. All systems will receive their signals from domestic

communications satellites placed high enough in space so
that a national network show could be bounced off a satellite
direct to any CATV antenna in the country. While the sheer
wiring up of the country may take years, the real problem
may be to assemble enough lawyers to deal with all the com-
plications and disputes the transition will produce.

The principal dispute at the moment is between the
burgeoning CATV industry and the broadcasting companies,
whose network systems and local stations CATV threatens.
While lobbying assiduously in Washington to slow down
the advance of the cable—the chief complaint is that cable
TV will inevitably lead to "pay TV" and viewers will have
to pay for what they now receive free—almost all of the major
broadcasters and networks have hedged their bets by
scrambling to buy up CATV franchises. All sorts of others
are getting into the act. Among those seeking a franchise for
the New York City borough of Queens are the New York
Times, David Susskind, labor mediator Theodore W. Kheel,
TelePrompTer Corporation and the Jamaica Water
Company. . . .

But the "real magic" of the coaxial cable . . . is its two-
way capability. With switching equipment installed in the
system, the now passive TV viewer will be able to send back
signals along the line. Homes could be connected to a central
computer for instant figuring of, say, income taxes. Housewives could examine merchandise projected on TV screens
and place orders by punching a couple of buttons. Pollsters
could obtain immediate reactions to TV shows, or commercials, or even political candidates. Politicians could obtain
an accurate consensus from their constituents on important
public issues.

At a corporate level, Dr. Peter Goldmark, head of CBS
Laboratories, suggests that big companies could divide themselves into small units scattered around the countryside in
smaller cities and towns, with all units connected by cable or
laser beam. Using picture phones, instant memorandum
printers, big-screen television for conferences, and computer

circuits providing information at the touch of a button, the company could operate just as well as if everyone were in the same building. It might even operate better, since employees could live closer to work, in pleasant surroundings, and feel like members of a team rather than cogs in a giant corporate machine.

The real millennium will be in education. The cable will open up hundreds of new channels that could be used for adult-education broadcasts — for example, language or remedial-reading courses directed at the residents of urban ghettos. [For a detailed discussion of this possibility, see "The Potential of Cable TV" in Section II of this compilation. —Ed.] In classrooms the TV-computer link will produce a fantastic proliferation of "information retrieval" systems, such as the one now in experimental operation at Oklahoma's Oral Roberts University. Here students can sit in front of individual TV sets in library carrels and press buttons to order showings of taped or filmed programs from the library's "electronic shelves."

Corporations are at present engaged in stiff competition to see who will provide the hardware for these incipient delights. One organization with much at stake is the telephone company. Bell has not been especially pleased to see the introduction, by CATV-system operators, of a *second* communications wire into the home, especially when the CATV cable has many times the electronic capacity of a telephone wire. The telephone company is now attempting to convince CATV-system builders to lease Bell-manufactured CATV equipment instead of buying it independently. This enables the telephone company to retain control. Bell Labs is experimenting with coaxial-cable designs with greatly increased signal-carrying capacity. RCA engineers, meanwhile, are cranking up experimental transmission frequencies as high as 100 billion cycles per second that can be modulated to carry enormous quantities of information.

An End to Network Dominance?

But the most important question is: Who is going to end up producing the TV programs? The creation of many more channels will mean that the three great networks of "affiliated" TV stations will no longer be able to count on occupying a quasi-monopolistic position on the public airways and dividing up the viewing public more or less among themselves. The networks will still originate programs for national advertisers to sponsor, but these programs will have to compete with those on dozens of other channels: commercial shows produced by independent stations organized in smaller rival networks, public educational broadcasts, pay-TV presentations, locally sponsored programs originated by the CATV systems themselves. (Many CATV systems already produce their own programs, from televised PTA meetings to concerts and first-run movies. But the purpose is primarily to lure new subscribers.) Advertisers might be especially interested in dealing with the CATV-system owner; by switching a few knobs, the system operator could send different commercials to different sections of town, and advertisers could obtain precise results on marketing effectiveness.

Of all of these miscellaneous corporate interests bidding for pieces of the CATV pie, it is impossible to predict who will originate and pay for what, who will have a right to what. However, the presumed future breakup of the major networks, or at least the prospect of a proliferation of competing channels, is being welcomed, perhaps somewhat prematurely, by such TV critics as former CBS news chief Fred Friendly, now a TV consultant for the Ford Foundation. It is his contention that the networks are sheltered by the Government from the kind of competition that might stimulate them to improve program quality, and at the same time are locked in a soul-deadening competition for the mass audiences that encourages them to appeal to the lowest common denominator of taste.

Broadcasters tend to classify these opinions as somewhere between intellectual snobbery and aggravated assault, and insist that the age of the cable will be somewhat less than glorious. Though many CATV operators maintain cable TV is uniquely suited to give local areas indigenous programing, a report titled *Television and the Wired City,* financed by the National Association of Broadcasters, concludes that CATV stations would merely be funnels for "nationally produced and disseminated mass entertainment," with no sense of responsibility to their communities. The report warns that "significant social values" may be lost if "community institutions" (i.e., local TV stations) are allowed to be displaced by what it darkly refers to as the "wire grid."

The only recent national television policy of any kind was created in 1967 with the passage of the Public Broadcasting Act. It established a corporation which will provide financial assistance to local stations for cultural, educational and public-service broadcasts. Though initially plagued by lack of funds, noncommercial TV could, by developing audience tastes for material that now seems riskily noncommercial, become the catalyst for the general upgrading of programing that Friendly and others hope to see.

Do-It-Yourself TV

If CATV, the broadcasters and the Government become hopelessly enmeshed in a totally unproductive imbroglio, the viewer who is dissatisfied may have one out: do-it-yourself TV. In a sense this is already here in the form of still rather expensive home-TV tape recorders. If you are bored with Lucy's or Doris Day's kids, why not watch your neighbor's?

An even more important device will be the videograph, or whatever name is eventually coined for records that register a picture as well as sound. The system that is closest at hand is called EVR—Electronic Video Recording—invented by CBS's Dr. Peter Goldmark, who also invented the long-playing record. EVR is a system for manufacturing special film cartridges that, using a special player attachment on the TV set, can be played like records. A cartridge of EVR film, one half inch thick and seven inches in diameter, can carry almost an hour of black-and-white programing or a half hour of color.

CBS will begin marketing EVR cartridges next year [1969] to schools (where it has a huge potential as a means of mass education) and to TV stations (as a less expensive substitute for videotape). The price is still too high for the average consumer—about $400 for a player attachment selling to the educational community, and $20-$100 for each program cartridge, depending on length and content—but a vast home market should be in sight as soon as CBS brings the cost down. The resulting boom could conceivably produce in just a few years a giant new video-record industry as big as the present $780 million phonograph-record industry, and perhaps seriously challenge live television by occupying great stretches of millions of viewers' available viewing time.

The real beauty of EVR is that it entails almost none of the perplexing troubles facing use of the airways or coaxial cables. As in the phonograph-record business, almost anyone can get into the business overnight and, if his product is good enough, make a success. Anything, potentially, could be readily available. Which brings us back to our original question: What do we really want out of television?

As society consumes more and more entertainment in huge volume [notes the report on *Television and the Wired City*], it becomes increasingly difficult to satisfy or even to interest audiences. The appetite-jading process is unavoidably intensified by television more than by any other medium simply because of its central position in the average citizen's life.

Jaded beyond recall with a four-day work week and lots of time to kill, it may be that we will turn to TV for ever more exotic escapism and more titillating titillation and let it go at that, leaving its real potentials untapped. If such is the case, it might be inaccurate to say that it is what we "want," but it would not be unfair to say it is what we deserve.

THE IMPACT ON TOMORROW'S WORLD [2]

When the first telegram was delivered to the British Foreign Office in the 1840's the Foreign Secretary, Lord Palmerston, read it and declared: "My God, this is the end of diplomacy." Hyperbole aside, his reaction was sound. He recognized, with the instinct of a threatened man, the impending influence of mass communications on his world of personal statecraft.

Today, looking towards the 1970's, another change in communications patterns, as influential as the one which dismayed Palmerston, may have a comparable effect on present-day diplomacy.

Granted it is a long leap between Palmerston's telegram and today's satellites, in comparison the communications leap during the next dozen years will be even longer and more dramatic. In the 1970's, by conservative estimate, communications facilities will double. Paced by satellites, for the first time, a network will connect all parts of the globe with all types of communication—telephone, telegraph, radio, television, facsimile, or information storage and retrieval.

But this is only part of the story. The many communications links of satellites will be spectacular, but they are only the passive framework for transferring information. Beyond the mechanics of the network, there is a larger prospect opened to everyone. This prospect, until very recently a Utopian one, is the creation of a world-information-grid which will make possible the transfer of man's accumulated knowledge throughout the globe.

This development coincides with that tremendous expansion in knowledge resources which is known as the information explosion. Between now and 1980 the amount of *additional* information to be collected, stored, and distributed will be equal in volume to all the data produced in the 2000 years of prior human history.

[2] From "American Diplomacy and a Changing Technology," by Leonard H. Marks, former director of the United States Information Agency. *Television Quarterly.* 7:5-14. Spring '68. Reprinted by permission.

Coming: Worldwide Television

Despite the present electronic sophistication, information links with the rest of the world have been sporadic. Until now books and periodicals have been the major transmitters of information. Overseas electronic circuits—telephone, teletype, and radio—have been limited largely to the North Atlantic area. Except for radio, the United States has not had circuits connecting it directly with over 70 per cent of the world's population in Africa, South America or (until early this year) the Asian mainland. In fact, these three continents have had few direct telecommunications links among themselves.

The new information grid will overcome such limitations dramatically. The grid will be "anchored" to the high-flying communications satellites that can transmit voice, visual, or printed information in any amount to anyplace.

The most publicized aspect of the new grid has been the potential of worldwide television. Although it has glamorous appeal, television will play a relatively insignificant part in the grid's activities; essentially television will transmit such occasional "world events" as Olympics, the election of a Pope, or an American presidential inauguration.

The grid's day-to-day chores will involve less spectacular transmissions. Many of these will involve the commonplace telephone. Today, most of the world's telephones are in the United States; during the next decade, the balance will shift abroad. The telephone will become the most important single medium in the new world communications grid, followed by telex networks. These networks, capable of high-speed transmissions, will be able to handle any kind of printed data, from today's stock quotations to entire books. In one 1962 experiment, the "primitive" Telstar satellite handled data at the rate of 1.5 million words a minute, or the equivalent of transmitting the entire 66 books of the Bible every 30 seconds.

Over the long term, however, the greatest impact on the new world-information-grid may be made by the computer and related information-retrieval devices. The grid will be most efficient when it is transferring information at high speeds from one electronic storage source to another. Since computers offer the only hope of storing the flood of new information data produced every year, they promise to emerge as the libraries of the world-information-grid—making their information available instantaneously to other computer libraries throughout the earth. Computers will be, in their way, the new Library of Congress, Vatican Library, British Museum and all our hometown Carnegie libraries rolled into one, serving a worldwide clientele.

The popular-science writers have made us generally aware of these prospects. However, we have only recently begun to consider the effect of making the world's recorded knowledge available to everyone. This revolutionary prospect for the information grid will be an important (perhaps decisive) new element in our world as we approach the next century. The grid is not a far-off, science-fiction fantasy; it is being formed now, and it will be substantially in place by 1975. Moreover, the United States is linked inextricably to its success—or its failure. American technology is creating the grid; American sources will provide a large part of the information flowing through it.

Impact of the World Grid

With all its capabilities, the grid can play a vital role in creating a more viable world order. Properly utilized, it could:

—strengthen the advanced economies of Western Europe and Japan through an efficient sharing of scientific and other information. It will modify, in part, the divisive effects of the so-called technological gap.

—speed up the development process throughout Asia, Africa, and Latin America through the programed input of a wide range of technical information tailored to local problems.

—be a powerful instrument for encouraging "bridge-building" contacts with Eastern Europe and the Soviet Union.

—strengthen American society through the more efficient transmittal and storage of information from abroad. . . .

The grid's greatest weakness is the present critical shortage of domestic communications facilities throughout the world. For example, it often takes several years to get a new telephone installed in countries such as France or Brazil; in small and less-developed countries, a telephone is frequently just a status symbol and an object of great curiosity. There will be no advantage in having satellites relay long-distance calls if these calls cannot be connected to circuits within the country receiving the message. The problem is, of course, most acute in the developing countries of Asia and Africa where the need for communications is greater.

To understand the American role in the grid's development, it is necessary to consider the changes that communications are having on our own national style at home. Increasingly, the United States is a society oriented to the collection, storage and distribution of knowledge—from the evening news by radio or TV to the computer facility at MIT. This phenomenon was first described by Princeton's Dr. Fritz Machlup several years ago in his book, *The Production and Distribution of Knowledge in the United States*. Dr. Machlup's rough measure of the U.S. economy as an information-servicing mechanism was startling.

He estimated that, in 1958, the measurable U.S. "knowledge industry" spent $136 billion, or nearly 30 per cent of the Gross National Product. This is impressive enough; but his more important finding was that the production and distribution of information of all kinds—from schoolhouse to Random House—was growing at twice the rate of the over-all economy. In 1965, the editors of *Fortune* confirmed this in a study updating Professor Machlup's figures, and estimated that, by 1963, the nation's total outlay for knowledge had reached $195 billion, up 43 per cent in five years. The effort accounted for the employment of 24 million persons, or 36 per cent of the nonfarm labor force.

The "knowledge industry" is even bigger and more booming these days, with no signs of a letup, and the nature of the industry is changing radically. When Professor Machlup made his original estimates, he defined the knowledge industry in traditional terms—the educational system, the mass media, book publishing, libraries, and so forth. Today's knowledge is being reshaped by the possibilities of electronic storage and retrieval of information, using computers and other automated devices. Information-grids linking these devices are being formed every day; within the next half-dozen years a national information-grid, integrating these small grids, will be in place.

Key Role for America

More and more, as a nation of fact-gatherers and distributors, the United States spills out this enthusiasm over its borders. The American share in the world's knowledge industry assures it a special role which is too big to ignore. Sixty-five per cent of all world communications originate in this country. This is matched by a long lead in the production of information. A rough but useful indicator of this, of course, is the well-documented disparity in research spending throughout the world. In dollar terms, the American effort is twice that of the Soviet Union, three times that of all of Western Europe and, in most of the rest of the world, the gap becomes a chasm.

This, in summary, is the environment in which America's role in the development of the world-information-grid will be played. The conditions which brought it to this long lead are varied, but they are largely the result of the increasingly sophisticated national commitment to the "knowledge industry," reflecting the vision of the United States as a problem-solving society.

Nevertheless, our information lead has created problems overseas. A preview of this is found in the current debate over the "technological gap" between Europe and this country. This subject has many facets, but the one of most concern has been the heavy political overtone of the debate. The facts are shoved aside by the emotionally charged image of an American technological monolith, moving in on "poor but honest" European hand-crafters. It is a caricature which combines political, economic, and cultural imperialism in one neat, unattractive package. More of it will be seen in the coming years, stirring up fear of American "domination" not only in Europe but in less affluent areas which are just beginning to grapple with this century's technology.

The output of our national knowledge industry is, of course, a tremendous resource. A problem occurs as this resource produces at a rate that is disparate with that of the rest of the world. If anything, the gap can be expected to widen in the coming years. America must examine this prospect and decide on a strategy to deal with it.

What, in fact, are the alternatives? The answer does not lie in slowing down. With unresolved economic and social problems here at home and abroad, conscientious thinking should plan the role that United States information resources can play in strengthening the prospects for world stability.

This strategy will have to be adapted to a great variety of situations abroad. Information-transfer arrangements with an African country that has 90 per cent illiteracy, 200 college graduates, and almost no domestic communications will be quite different from those with Sweden and its total literacy and well-developed higher education system.

Overseas, Impact Will Vary

Western Europe and Japan present the most immediate opportunities for the world-information-grid. The Europeans and the Japanese are both increasingly sensitive to the importance of information storage and transfer network, similar to the one now evolving in this country.

The Europeans' success in this project will depend, in part, on their ability to modify a number of present restrictive attitudes. One is the lingering tradition of secretiveness in their research-and-development work. Another is the nationalistic inhibition in sharing regional information resources. It would be unfortunate if these attitudes held up formation of the network, since Europeans, over the long run, cannot think in terms of "Italian research" or "Norwegian research" any more than they are able to make a distinction between research done in California or New Jersey.

There is every reason to encourage the Europeans to overcome these problems. The American information-transfer network should be linked directly into their regional system, permitting a broader exchange of information. This will not completely eradicate the mutual "technology gap" problems, which are based on other factors besides information transfer. It should, however, take everyone a long way towards equalizing the present imbalance of information resources and certainly . . . lower the present level of tension on this subject.

If the Europeans and Japanese are strong in this area it will insure their continued domestic economic health, and make available their informational resources in the common effort to step up the developmental pace in Asia, Africa, and Latin America. The most immediate prospects are in those developing countries which are approaching the point of economic and social take-off, ready to move from a subsistence economy towards full development. Success in this field depends largely on the skill with which they can apply information resources supplied by the grid to their local problems, whether it involves building an oil refinery or an elementary-school system. There has never been an opportunity to explore the role that full access to data resources could play in situations like this. The new grid opens up this possibility in ways that could dramatically affect development prospects in these take-off countries.

The situation is more complex in those countries which have no immediate hope for a take-off of any kind. It begins with a critical lack of managers and technicians trained to use information to handle the problems, from undercapitalization to overpopulation, in which they are enmeshed. Flooding them with facts and figures from the information grid could be worse than useless. They need telephones before they can use satellites; they need adding machines before they can use computers. And yet the grid has a role to play in these situations, if its facilities are used flexibly to supply data directly relevant to local conditions. Information systems can be adapted around these needs, with the ability to step up their capacity as the development process gains greater momentum.

Impact on World Diplomacy

Communist countries present another interesting challenge as the information grid develops. It is doubtful that the largest of them, mainland China, will join the grid soon. The Soviet and the East European regimes will probably view the grid in a different light. There is no question that they will be interested in its benefits, but it is doubtful that they will want to contribute usefully to an exchange of data. The difficulty comes in their desire to pick-and-choose. They will want to share the technological data that will flow through the grid, but they will be less enthusiastic about making available to their people the grid's other products such as uncensored news and information about the outside world. The United States, in turn, needs to make it clear that it is prepared to share its information resources with them on the basis of reciprocity. The result could be a major contribution to our "bridge-building" efforts with Eastern Europe and the Soviet Union.

These are some of the possibilities. Each deserves careful attention. However, the information grid does not give the chance to score easy international points. America's foreign prospects are not going to be magically improved by accelerated information-transfer techniques. The grid does not promise instant Utopia. What it does offer is the opportunity to bring human intelligence more directly to bear on major world problems.

During the next half dozen years, the grid will be taking shape. How will it affect the ways in which America deals with the rest of mankind? The answer does not come easily, since this is . . . a quantum jump which is not merely an expansion in mechanical communications but an expansion in the psychological horizons of individuals all over the world.

Nevertheless, some effects of the information grid can be anticipated. One of them will involve America's diplomacy. Lord Palmerston may have been dismayed by the introduction of the telegram into diplomacy, but he might take some posthumous comfort in the fact that, over a century later, there has not been much progress beyond the telegram in our own diplomatic communications. Diplomatic information, as in Palmerston's time, is still stored on individual pieces of paper stuffed into files—or in the errant memories of men.

The information grid promises transformation of traditional diplomacy. At one level, it will make practical a system for collecting and storing all of the bits of factual information which form the raw material of diplomacy into computers for retrieval on command. The foreign-affairs expert's time can be devoted more profitably to value judgments of the information at hand, rather than on time-consuming effort in collecting the information itself.

At another level, the information grid opens the possibility of direct sight-and-sound consultation between the State Department and its embassies. The prospect is no panacea: instantaneous communications do not guarantee instantaneous wisdom. But there are equal dangers in maintaining the pretense of leisurely diplomacy in today's world. Thomas Jefferson could complain mildly that he had not heard from one of his ambassadors for a year, but he lived in an era where only a half dozen countries were important to America and where 90 per cent of the world's population had no influence on its interests. Today, any political event abroad has its seismic influence on American interests, and it is better knowing about it sooner than later.

People-to-People Contact

Diplomatic traffic will be only a small part of the new grid's traffic. The grid will have an even greater effect on our foreign relations through its tremendous capability for allowing more men to trade more ideas across national boundaries than has ever been possible. The effects of this people-to-people contact are literally incalculable. If one lesson has been learned, it is the invincible tendency of the experts to underestimate people's desire to communicate, once the channels are open, for all kinds of purposes—from business deals to exchanging birthday greetings.

Although the United States will be only one of 100 or more nations in the grid, it has a special role in seeing that it develops in ways that serve these needs. One of these roles should be to insure that the grid is available to all nations and their citizens. In proposing the satellite communications network, the United States declared that it should be open to every nation belonging to International Telecommunications Union—58 nations share the ownership and operation of that satellite system. The same spirit of openness should pervade the information grid.

The idea that the grid needs to be protected from censorship or "management" of information seems obvious to us. But there is a definite danger that other countries—not all of them Communist—may press for arrangements to screen unpleasant facts and ideas from the grid. The United States has had to argue against similar restrictions in international "freedom-of-information" agreements for many years. The new information grid should be rid of such censorship attempts.

The second area where the United States has an interest is in assuring everyone that the grid serves public as well as private information needs. Most of the messages sent through the grid will be private, and most of these will be commercial. This is, of course, an important function of the grid. It will have a major influence on world commerce, and it will insure the economic health of the grid itself. But the grid should also be used to connect noncommercial information sources throughout the world. These include universities, libraries, and research institutes. The effectiveness of these institutions depends largely upon adequate access to information beyond their walls. No longer can any one school or library be a repository for more than a fraction of the data its students and researchers need. The new grid can give them this access on a worldwide scale through electronic interchanges with similar institutions.

A World Commonwealth of Knowledge

This will not happen quickly, however, unless positive steps are taken to make it happen. The barriers involved are formidable, but the rewards are potentially too great to ignore. In the United States, it represents a challenge to its 2,000 universities and their allied institutions. The challenge is nothing less than expanding the spectrum of their scholarship to the entire world by receiving as well as contributing knowledge — a commonwealth of universities linked by electronics.

All of these prospects will affect America's world role in the 1970's in ways that one can only dimly perceive now. It is, however, clear that the United States' past tradition and future interests call for active American initiatives, both public and private, to assure the success of the world-information grid. It could be one of our most innovative steps in strengthening the prospects of a peaceful world community during the next decade.

BIBLIOGRAPHY

An asterisk (*) preceding a reference indicates that the article or a part of it has been reprinted in this book.

BOOKS, PAMPHLETS, AND DOCUMENTS

Blum, Eleanor. Reference books in the mass media. University of Illinois Press. '63.

Dale, Edgar. Can you give the public what it wants? Cowles. '67.

Danielson, W. A. and Wilhoit, G. C. Jr. A computerized bibliography of mass communications research, 1944-64. Magazine Publishers Association. 575 Lexington Ave. New York 10017. '67.

Dizard, W. P. Television; a world view. Syracuse University Press. '66.

Emery, Edwin and others. Introduction to mass communications. Dodd. '65.

Friendly, F. W. Due to circumstances beyond our control . . . . Random House. '67.

Gross, Gerald, ed. Publishers on publishing. Bowker. '61.

Hohenberg, John. The news media: a journalist looks at his profession. Holt. '68.

Klapper, J. T. The effects of mass communication. Free Press. '60.

Lacy, D. M. Freedom and communications. University of Illinois Press. '61.

Lang, Kurt, and Lang, G. E. Politics and television. Quadrangle. '68.

Machlup, Fritz. The production and distribution of knowledge in the United States. Princeton University Press. '62.

McLuhan, H. M. Understanding media; the extensions of man. McGraw. '64.

McLuhan, H. M. and Fiore, Quentin. The medium is the massage. Random House. '67.

*MacNeil, Robert. The people machine; the influence of television on American politics. Harper. '68.
    Adaptation. Harper's Magazine. 237:72-80. O. '68. News on TV and how it is unmade.

Markham, J. W. Voices of the Red giants; communications in Russia and China. Iowa State University Press. '67.

Montgomery, Robert. Open letter from a television viewer. Heineman. '68.

Neal, H. E. Communication: from stone age to space age. Messner. '60.

Opotowsky, Stan. TV: the big picture. Dutton. '61.

Peck, W. A. Anatomy of local radio-TV copy. G/L TAB Books. '68.

Peterson, Wilbur, comp. Organizations, publications and directories in the mass media of communications. School of Journalism. State University of Iowa. Iowa City. '60.

Rider, J. R. The student journalist and broadcasting. Rosen. '68.

Rivers, W. L. and Schramm, Wilbur. Responsibility in mass communication. rev. ed. Harper. '69.

Schramm, Wilbur, ed. Mass communications; a book of readings. University of Illinois Press. '60.

Schumach, Murray. The face on the cutting room floor; the story of movie and television censorship. Morrow. '64.

Seldes, G. V. The new mass media: challenge to a free society. Public Affairs Press. '68.

Skornia, H. J. and Kitson, J. W. eds. Problems and controversies in television and radio; basic readings. Pacific Books. '68.

Sopkin, Charles. Seven glorious days, seven fun-filled nights. Simon & Schuster. '68.

Stearn, G. E. ed. McLuhan: hot & cool. Dial. '67.

Steinberg, C. S. ed. Mass media and communication. Hastings House. '66.

Steinberg, Sigfrid. Five hundred years of printing. Criterion Books. '59.

Torre, Marie. Don't quote me. Doubleday. '65.

UNESCO. Mass media in the developing countries. (Reports and papers on mass communication, no 33) UNESCO Publications Center. 317 E. 34th St. New York 10016. '61.

United States. Congress. House of Representatives. Committee on Foreign Affairs. Subcommittee on International Organizations and Movements. Modern communications and foreign policy; report no 5 together with part 10 of the hearings (February 8-9, 1967) on winning cold war, U.S. ideological offensive. (House report no 362) 90th Congress, 1st session. Supt. of Docs. Washington, D.C. 20402. '67.

United States. Congress. House of Representatives. Committee on
Interstate and Foreign Commerce. Public broadcasting act of
1967; report to accompany H.R. 6736. (House report no 572)
90th Congress, 1st session. Supt. of Docs. Washington, D.C.
20402. '67.

United States. Congress. House of Representatives. Committee on
Interstate and Foreign Commerce. Subcommittee on Communications and Power. Subscription television; hearings, October 9-16, 1967. (Serial no 90-15) 90th Congress, 1st session.
Supt. of Docs. Washington, D.C. 20402. '67.

United States. Congress. Senate. Committee on the Judiciary. Subcommittee on Antitrust and Monopoly. The failing newspaper act; hearings: parts 1-4. July 12-August 15, 1967. 90th
Congress, 1st session. Supt. of Docs. Washington, D.C. 20402.
'67.

Walker, E. L. and Heyns, R. W. An anatomy for conformity.
Brooks/Cole. '67.

White, D. M. and Averson, Richard, comps. Sight, sound, and society; motion pictures and television in America. Beacon
Press. '68.

Williams, Raymond. Communications. rev. ed. Barnes & Noble.
'67.

Wyckoff, Gene. The image candidates; American politics in the
age of television. Macmillan. '68.

PERIODICALS

Advertising Age. 39:6. S. 16, '68. Better broadcasting group hits
continuing use of violence on TV.

Advertising Age. 39:96. S. 23, '68. House group asks FCC to again
delay pay TV approval.

Advertising Age. 39:118. S. 30, '68. N.Y. ghetto makes own TV
series aimed at building community pride.

Advertising Age. 39:134. S. 30, '68. FCC revives 50-50 rule; aims to
reduce network role in programming. S. E. Cohen.

Advertising Age. 39:1+. O. 14, '68. Find out why you're not reaching ghetto readers, newspapers advised. A. Allen.

Advertising Age. 39:144. O. 14, '68. FCC move seen in controversy
over CATV as medium.

America. 118:286. Mr. 2, '68. TV networks and Catholic broadcasting.
    Discussion: 118:389-90. Mr. 30, '68.

America. 118:308-9. Mr. 9, '68. Broadcasting and academicians.

America. 118:433. Ap. 6, '68. Television and race.

America. 118:454. Ap. 13, '68. Of many things; mass media in the nation's racial crisis. D. L. Flaherty.

America. 118:767. Je. 15, '68. Politics and television; suspension of equal-time proviso.

America. 119:7. Jl. 6, '68. Televised violence.

America. 119:639. D. 21, '68. TV access to Congress, justified by clear benefits.

American Educator. 4:18. F. '68. Review of the Public broadcasting act of 1967.

*Annals of the American Academy of Political and Social Science. 371:72-84. My. '67. The mass media—a need for greatness. André Fontaine.

*Annals of the American Academy of Political and Social Science. 378:68-74. Jl. '68. Impact of mass communications in America. W. C. Clark.

Atlantic. 221:96-9. My. '68. Radio free New York; WBAI. Alfred Mayor.

*Atlantic. 221:43-51. Je. '68. Media barons and the public interest. Nicholas Johnson.

Broadcasting. 75:44-5. S. 2, '68. TV as a backdrop in the ghetto home.

Broadcasting. 75:56. S. 2, '68. TV enters the space age next time up.

Broadcasting. 75:67-8. S. 9. '68. FCC wants action on pay-TV issue.

Broadcasting. 75:35. S. 16, '68. Rules that fell despite repairs.

Broadcasting. 75:38. S. 16, '68. House seeks delay on pay TV.

Broadcasting. 75:38+. S. 16, '68. Broadcasters' role as a social force.

Broadcasting. 75:64A. S. 16, '68. Threat of TV controls is seen.

Broadcasting. 75:34+. S. 23, '68. Electronics hold key to mass-media future.

Broadcasting. 75:48-9. S. 23, '68. Hoover hits TV violence.

Broadcasting. 75:52-3. S. 23, '68. TV's role in raising the caliber.

Broadcasting. 75:61. S. 23, '68. Fanning the fire under networks.

Broadcasting. 75:66. S. 23, '68. Little respect for media seen.

Broadcasting. 75:22. S. 30, '68. Radio's interest in TV standards.

Broadcasting. 75:40. S. 30, '68. No word left unspoken on violence.

Broadcasting. 75:44. O. 7, '68. Deep look at network clearances.

Broadcasting. 75:47-8. O. 7, '68. Cronkite defends TV's objectivity.

Broadcasting. 75:52. O. 21, '68. NATRA wants Negro on FCC.

Broadcasting. 75:60. O. 21, '68. Radio plays big role in adult lives.

Broadcasting. 75:62-3. O. 21, '68. TV violence problem probed in depth.

Broadcasting. 75:64. O. 21, '68. TV, bias and the news.

Business Week. p 23. F. 10, '68. Pay-TV's bad reception.

Business Week. p 110. F. 24, '68. Global TV tries a Spanish accent.

Business Week. p 112-14. Je. 1, '68. They keep U.S. travelers posted; American publishers of overseas English-language newspapers.

Business Week. p 110+. Je. 8, '68. Media get a message from Justice.

Business Week. p 44. Je. 15, '68. CATV gets a monitor.

Business Week. p 64-6. N. 2, '68. TV can't cover losses in covering the news.

Catholic World. 207:111-15. Je. '68. But what if McLuhan is right? Depaul Travers.

*Catholic World. 207:264-8. S. '68. Violence in the mass media. Solomon Simonson.

Changing Times. 22:44-7. Jl. '68. TV generation.

Christian Century. 85:385-8. Mr. 27, '68. Communications city. Robert Theobald.

Christian Century. 85:497-8. Ap. 17, '68. New approach to media is proposed. S. J. Rowland, Jr.

Christian Century. 85:672. My. 22, '68. Religious broadcasting; the graveyard ghetto.

Christian Century. 85:708-12. My. 29, '68. McLuhan, media and the ministry. T. A. Michael.

Christian Century. 85:1621-3. D. 25, '68. Educational technology and the church. C. A. Hewitt.

Christianity Today. 12:43-4. F. 16, '68. Political hang-ups for religious broadcasting.

Christianity Today. 12:48. My. 24, '68. Multi-medium man. H. B. Kuhn.

Christianity Today. 12:26-7. Ag. 16, '68. Guns of August; TV violence.

Columbia Journalism Review. 4:7-10. Winter '66. The sound of maturity. W. A. Wood.

Commentary. 45:69-71. Je '68. TV specials. Neil Compton.

*Commentary. 46:82-6. S. '68. Television and reality: violence for profit. Neil Compton.

Commonweal. 88:131-3. Ap. 19, '68. Tele-culture and the third world. N. P. Hurley.

Commonweal. 89:44-6. O. 11, '68. Equal time on radio and TV; Chicago Court of appeals finds FCC rulings unconstitutional. David Walker.

Dun's Review. 91:20+. F. '68. Need for subscription TV. J. S. Wright.

Editor & Publisher. 101:15+. Ag. 24, '68. Newspapers top TV for political news.

Editor & Publisher. 101:12+. S. 14, '68. Census bureau finds editorials disturbing.

Editor & Publisher. 101:15. S. 14, '68. Fortas puts privacy over press freedom. L. A. Hudson.

Editor & Publisher. 101:108. S. 28, '68. News format called outdated by psychologist.

Editor & Publisher. 101:24. O. 12, '68. General Hershey blasts news media.

Editor & Publisher. 101:62. O. 19, '68. Readership of features tops viewing.

Electronic News. 13:12. O. 21, '68. Top court leaves copyright over CATV up to Congress.

English Journal. 57:565-7+. Ap. '68. McLuhan thesis: its limits and its appeal; address, November 1967. Edward Lueders.

English Journal. 57:696-9. My. '68. Simultaneousness. J. S. Smith.

English Journal. 57:1326-9+. D. '68. Television and the teacher. C. S. Steinberg.

Financial World. 129:8+. Je. 5, '68. Communications—new horizons.

Foreign Affairs. 46:758-69. Jl. '68. Two revolutions. D. C. Smith, Jr.

Fortune. 78:145-6. Jl. '68. Demand side of communications. Max Ways.

Good Housekeeping. 166:193. Mr. '68. Should children's TV habits be controlled?

*Harper's Magazine. 234:45-52. Mr. '67. The real masters of television. Robert Eck.
    Same abridged: Reader's Digest. 90:78-82. My. '67. Why TV is the way it is.

Library Journal. 93:1729-32. Ap. 15, '68. Elimination of reading: a status report. G. N. Gordon.

Library Journal. 93:2064. My. 15, '68. TV to educate preschoolers.

Life. 64:18. Ap. 12, '68. Courage at last, or just bleeps? J. M. Ferrer, III.

Life. 65:6. Ag. 9, '68. Flawed breakthrough on blackness; Of black America. Doris Innis.

Media/Scope. 12:36-9+. Ag. '68. Violence on TV.

Media/Scope. 12:82-3. Ag. '68. Non-metro radio listening—from 72% to 1%.

Nation. 206:222. F. 12, '68. Television; excerpt from address, October 1959. E. R. Murrow.

Nation. 206:358. Mr. 11, '68. Television. John Horn.
    Reply with rejoinder: L. E. Spivak. 206:458+. Ap. 8, '68.

Nation. 206:375-9. Mr. 18, '68. Journalism on the air. Desmond Smith; Michael Harris.

Nation. 206:390. Mr. 18, '68. Television; Kerner commission on Negro neglect. John Horn.

Nation. 206:789-91. Je. 17, '68. Mask of objectivity. L. R. Colitt.

Nation. 206:824-6. Je. 24, '68. Broadcast oratory: fallacies of equal time. Sally Fly.

Nation. 207:115-16. Ag. 19, '68. Guns, Congress and the networks. Maurine Christopher.

*New Leader. 49:20-1. O. 10, '66. The McLuhan follies. Robert Meister.

*New Leader. 51:18-20. Mr. 25, '68. Case for TV journalism. Reuven Frank.

*New Republic. 157:7-8. D. 2, '67. The seedier media. David Sanford.

New Republic. 158:32-5. Ap. 27, '68. Issue versus image. Patrick Anderson.

New Republic. 158:4. Je. 1, '68. T.R.B. from Washington; CBS report, Hunger in America.

New Republic. 158:41-3. Je. 8. '68. Color us black; failure of commercial TV to report adequately on race relations and ghetto problems. Ed Dowling.

New Republic. 158:13-15. Je. 15, '68. Why not ban paid political broadcasting? John Osborne.

New Republic. 159:21-2. Jl. 27, '68. Television: concerning Of Black America series. Ed Dowling.

New Republic. 159:16-17. O. 5, '68. Right of reply; FCC's personal attack rules held unconstitutional by Chicago Federal court. Simon Lazarus.

New York Times. p 1+. O. 8, '68. Ratings to bar some films to children. Vincent Canby.

*New York Times. p 64. N. 11, '68. Black radio stations send soul and service to millions. R. E. Dallos.

New York Times. p 1+. D. 10, '68. Panel would lift curbs on cable TV. J. W. Finney.

*New York Times. p 24. D. 30, '68. Radio and suburbs discover each other. Robert Windeler.

New York Times. p 52. F. 16, '69. TV men worry over license renewal. Christopher Lydon.

New York Times. p 1+. F. 28, '69. New role for F.C.C.: arbiter of revolution in TV and radio. Jack Gould.

New York Times. p 95. Mr. 12, '69. A Federal department of communications is urged. Jack Gould.

New York Times. p 79. Mr. 17, '69. Pastore's plan to preview shows alarms networks. Jack Gould.

*New York Times Magazine. p 18-19+. Ja. 29, '67. Understanding McLuhan (in part). Richard Kostelanetz.

*New York Times Magazine. p 25+. Mr. 12, '67. A program for Public-TV. Lester Markel.

*New York Times Magazine. p 28-9+. Je. 11, '67. What's wrong with American newspapers? A. H. Raskin.

New York Times Magazine. p 34-5+. My. 26, '68. Deadlier than a western; the battle over cable TV. R. L. Smith.

New York Times Magazine. p 5+. Jl. 14, '68. Since the kiddies are hooked, why not use TV for a Head Start program? John Leonard.

New Yorker. 44:107-8+. Mr. 2, '68. The air [corporation for public broadcasting]. M. J. Arlen.

New Yorker. 44:34-42+. Ag. 3, '68. Profiles: Huntley and Brinkley. William Whitworth.

Newsweek. 71:58. Mr. 4, '68. Making it, underground.

Newsweek. 71:87. Mr. 11, '68. White on black; effect of mass media on riots.

Newsweek. 71:108. Mr. 11, '68. Cronkite takes a stand.

Newsweek. 71:93-4. Mr. 18, '68. Antismoke signals.

Newsweek. 71:67. Ap. 1, '68. Brightening the boob tube; children's television workshop for pre-schoolers.

Newsweek. 71:57. Ap. 29, '68. Race and restraint.

Newsweek. 71:61. Je. 10, '68. Where the action isn't; political reporters attracted by crowds.

Newsweek. 71:100. Je. 10, '68. Hunger pains; hunger in America.

Newsweek. 72:78-9. Jl. 1, '68. Court and cable.

Newsweek. 72:76. Jl. 8, '68. Notes from underground; members of underground press invade television program.

Newsweek. 72:74-5. Jl. 15, '68. Race race; black-oriented series and specials.

Newsweek. 72:56. Jl. 22, '68. Good-by, hambone; white newspaper coverage of the black ghetto.

Newsweek. 72:46. D. 30, '68. TViolence: hearings of President's commission on violence.

PTA Magazine. 62:32-3. Mr. '68. Time out for television.

Parents' Magazine. 43:58-9+. F. '68. Best on TV; choosing good programs for children. Frank Orme.

*Public Interest. p 52-66. Summer '68. Toward a modest experiment in cable television. Stephen White.

Public Relations Journal. 24:10-11. Je. '68. Communicating with a segmented society. P. Lesly.

Public Utilities Fortnightly. 82:69-74. S. 12, '68. Communications and computers: how shall the twain meet? B. Strassburg.

Publishers' Weekly. 193:72-3. Ja. 29, '68. Needs of educational TV explained to rights group.

Publishers' Weekly. 194:28. Jl. 1, '68. High court assures CATV free use of materials.

Reader's Digest. 92:115-17. F. '68. Transistor speaks around the world.

*Saturday Evening Post. 241:38-9+. N. 30, '68. Tomorrow's many-splendored tune-in. Sandford Brown.

Saturday Review. 51:3. Ja. 20, '68. Equal + equal = nothing. Goodman Ace.

Saturday Review. 51:92. Mr. 9, '68. Smooth surface; troubled waters. R. L. Shayon.

Saturday Review. 51:76. Mr. 16, '68. Invisible majority; student news out of perspective. Paul Woodring.

Saturday Review. 51:56. Mr. 23, '68. New test of the fairness doctrine. R. L. Shayon.

Saturday Review. 51:6. Ap. 13, '68. War is TV. Goodman Ace.

Saturday Review. 51:49. Ap. 20, 36. My. 25, '68. Julia: breakthrough or letdown? first family-type situation comedy about Negroes. R. L. Shayon.

Saturday Review. 51:42. My. 4, '68. Radio, God, and mammon; rescheduling Sunday programs. R. L. Shayon.

Saturday Review. 51:67-8+. My. 11, '68. Letter from a Vineyard editor; the weekly. H. B. Hough.

Saturday Review. 51:63-4. Je. 8, '68. On the hour every hour; sex and violence in U.S. programs. R. L. Tobin.

Saturday Review. 51:70-1. Je. 8, '68. Newest TV boom: Spanish-language stations. John Tebbel.

Saturday Review. 51:37. Je. 15, '68. Fairness doctrine. R. L. Shayon.

Saturday Review. 51:7. Je. 29, '68. Costly and equal time. Goodman Ace.

Saturday Review. 51:53-4. Jl. 13, '68. On the hour every hour; plans to curtail violence. R. L. Tobin.

Saturday Review. 51:60. Jl. 13, '68. Government-media conflict; how the news media handled the 1967 riots. Hillier Krieghbaum.

Senior Scholastic. 92:sup 16-17. Mr. 21, '68. Multimedia can reach and teach; Of Cabbages and Kings TV series in Detroit junior high schools. Delores Minor and Ethel Tincher.

Senior Scholastic. 92:Scholastic Teacher 4. Ap. 11, '68. TV for pre-schoolers. S. Holzman.

Senior Scholastic. 92:12-13. My. 2, '68. Equal T.V. time for all candidates: windfall or pitfall?

*Television Quarterly. 7:5-14. Spring '68. American diplomacy and a changing technology. L. H. Marks.

Time. 91:55. Ja. 26, '68. Not in the same league; coverage by three networks.

Time. 91:60. Ap. 19, '68. Responsibility amid emotion; comments after assassination of Martin Luther King.

Time. 91:74. My. 24, '68. Black on the channels.

Time. 91:65. Je. 21, '68. Catharsis, maybe; efforts to de-emphasize violence in programs.

Time. 91:55. Je. 28, '68. Victory for CATV.

Time. 92:84. O. 4, '68. Newsmagazine of the air; 60 minutes.

Time. 92:58. D. 27, '68. Fighting violence; network presidents defended TV.

Time. 92:58-9. D. 27, '68. Payday, some day; first nationwide and permanent pay-TV service authorized by FCC.

Time. 93:51. Ja. 3, '69. Pacification by attrition; investigation by National Commission on the Causes and Prevention of Violence.

Trans-Action. 5:39-45. My. '68. Best way to get more varied TV programs. H. J. Barnett and Edward Greenberg.

U.S. News & World Report. 64:28-9. Mr. 4, '68. Living-room war: impact of TV; people's reactions.

U.S. News & World Report. 65:67. D. 30, '68. Preview of pay television.

Vital Speeches of the Day. 34:242-5. F. 1, '68. Changing world: communicate, learn and understand; address, January 4, '68. H. I. Romnes.

Vital Speeches of the Day. 34:407-10. Ap. 15, '68. News media; address, February 27, 1968. J. C. Daly.

Vital Speeches of the Day. 34:469-72. My. 15, '68. Communications revolution; address, February 11, 1968. Hoyt Ammidon.

*Vital Speeches of the Day. 34:605-8. Jl. 15, '68. Future of communication; address, May 15, 1968. L. A. Hyland.

Vogue. 151:44. F. 15, '68. Ear-splitting underground press. John Gruen.